EASY ORGAN

BROADWAY CLASSICS

ISBN 0-634-06968-3

HAL•LEONARD®
CORPORATION
7777 W. BLUEMOUND RD. P.O. BOX 13819 MILWAUKEE, WI 53213

Visit Hal Leonard Online at
www.halleonard.com

CONTENTS

Bali Ha'i

from SOUTH PACIFIC

Electronic Organs

Upper: Hawaiian Guitar Preset
Lower: Flute (or Tibia) 8'
Pedal: 8'
Vib./Trem.: Vibrato On

Tonebar Organs

Upper: Hawaiian Guitar Preset or
         00 5160 300 Sustain, Add Percuss
Lower: (00) 4200 000
Pedal: 05
Vib./Trem.: Vibrato On

Lyrics by Oscar Hammerstein II
Music by Richard Rodgers

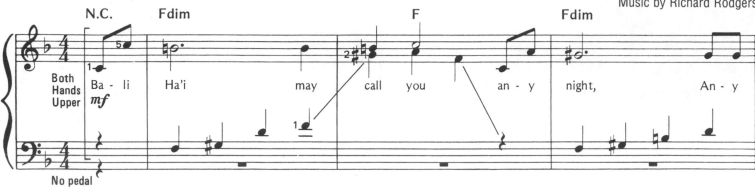

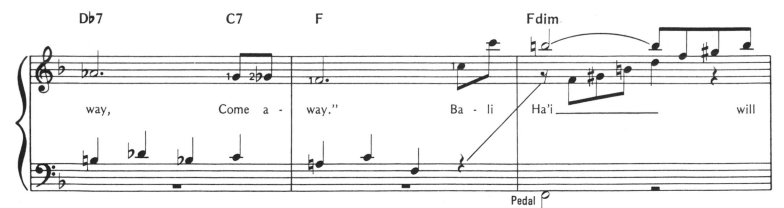

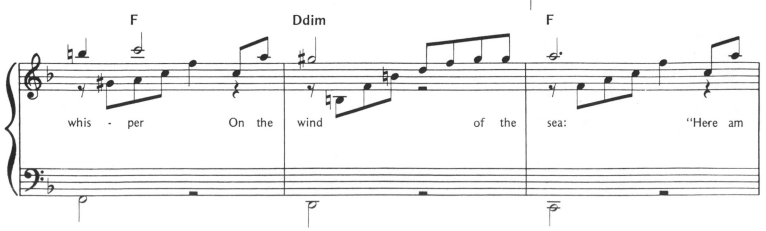

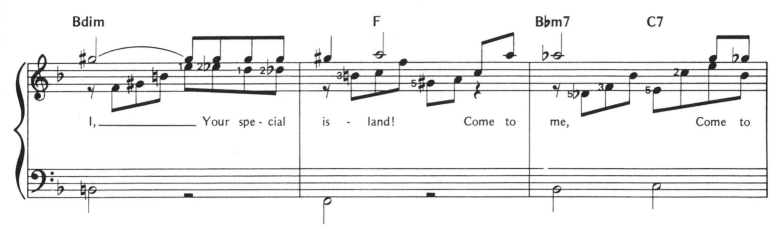

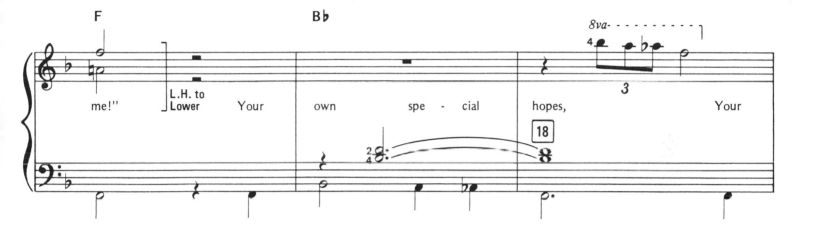

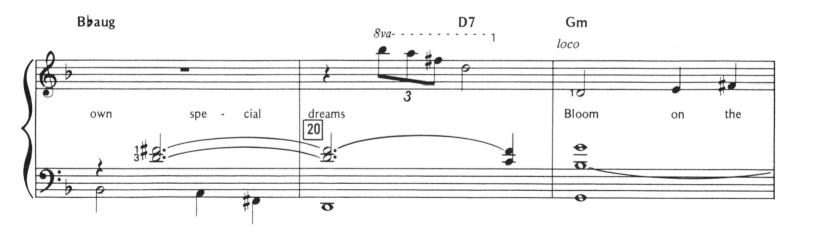

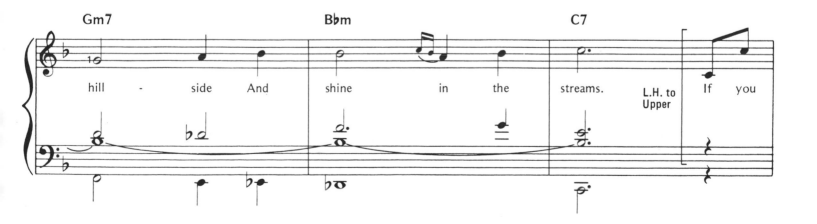

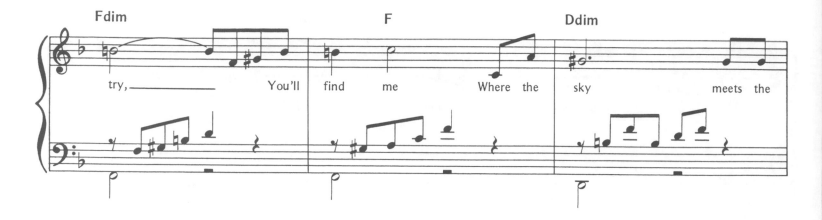

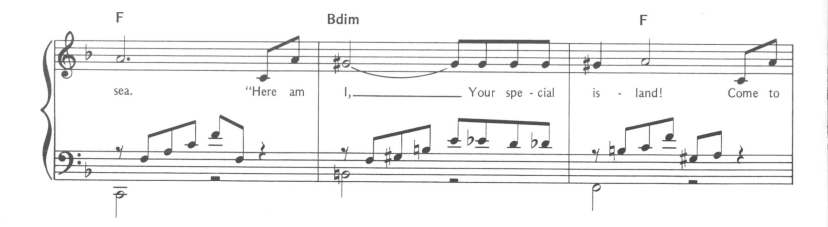

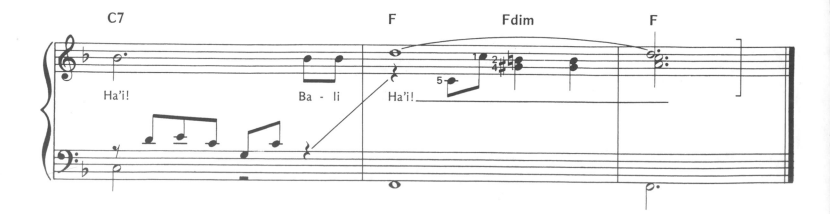

Bewitched

from PAL JOEY

Electronic Organs

Upper: Vibes Preset
Lower: Flute (or Tibia) 8′, Horn 8′
Pedal: String Bass
Vib./Trem.: On, Fast

Tonebar Organs

Upper: Vibes Preset or
        80 0600 100 Sustain, Add Percuss
Lower: (00) 5323 100
Pedal: String Bass
Vib./Trem.: On, Fast

Words by Lorenz Hart
Music by Richard Rodgers

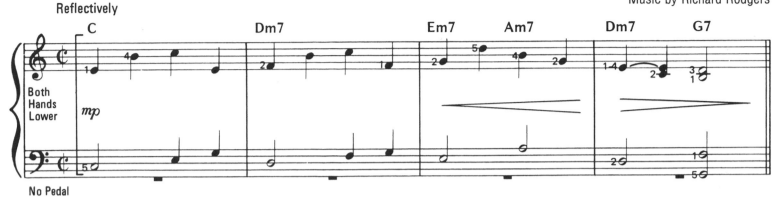

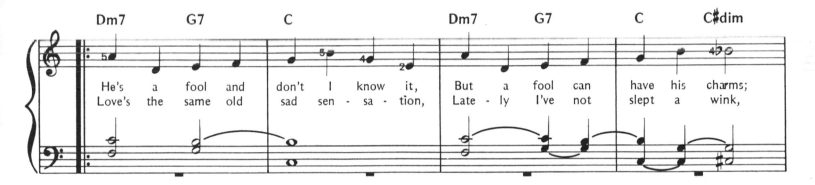

He's a fool and   don't I know it,   But a fool can   have his charms;
Love's the same old   sad sen - sa - tion,   Late - ly I've not   slept a wink,

I'm in love and   don't I show it,   Like a babe in   arms.
Since this half - pint   im - i - ta - tion,   Put me on the

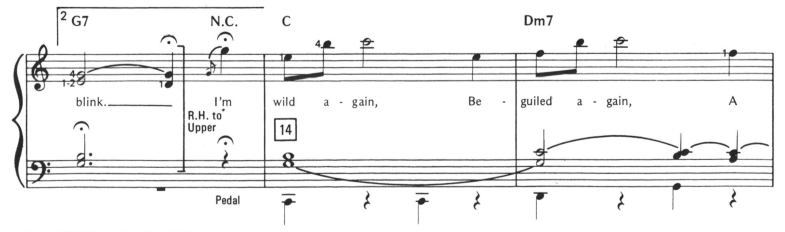

blink.   I'm   wild a - gain,   Be - guiled a - gain,   A
R.H. to
Upper

8

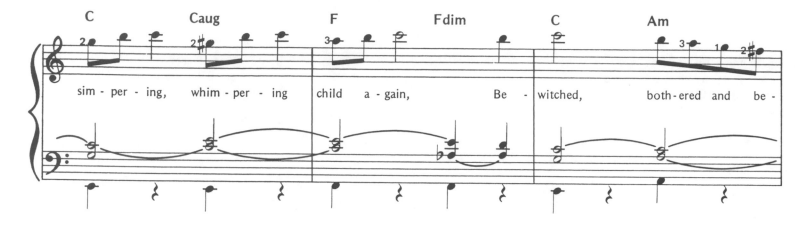

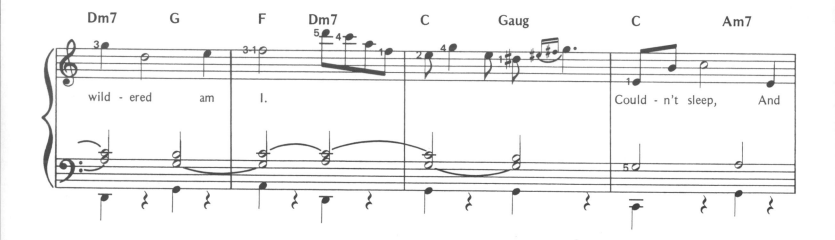

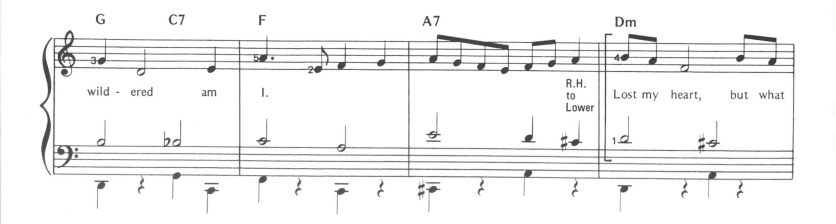

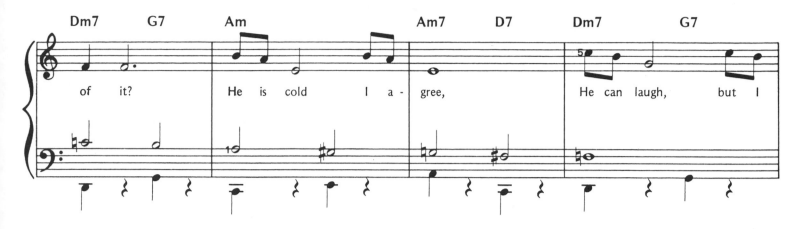

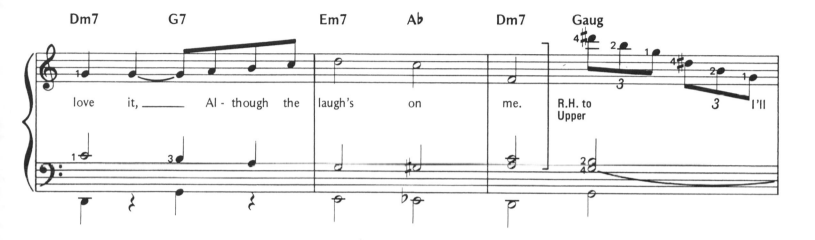

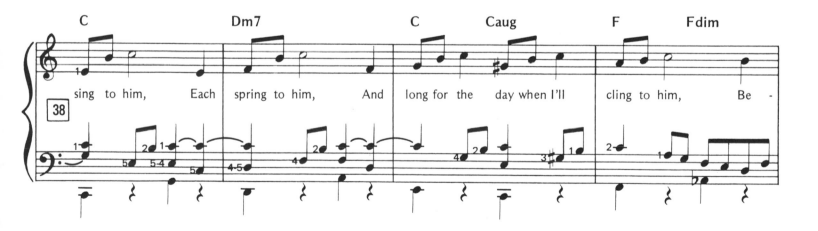

Cabaret

from the Musical CABARET

Electronic Organs

Upper: Flutes (or Tibias) 16', 8', 2'
        Brass 8'
Lower: Diapason 8', Flute 8'
        String 4'
Pedal: 16', 8', Sustain
Vib./Trem.: On, Full

Drawbar Organs

Upper: 60 8080 400
Lower: (00) 8654 310
Pedal: 68, Sustain
Vib./Trem.: On, Full

Words by Fred Ebb
Music by John Kander

Moderately

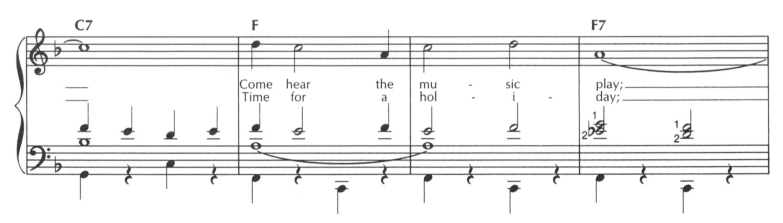

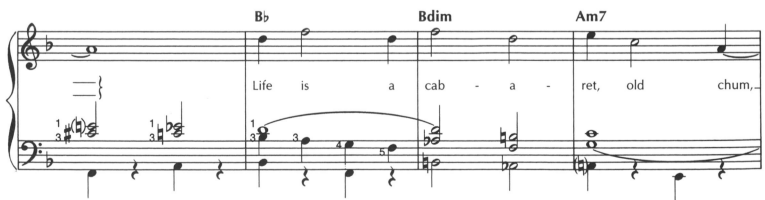

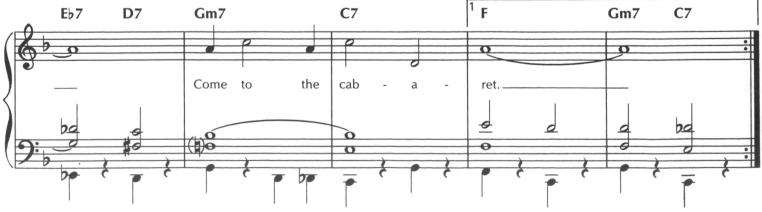

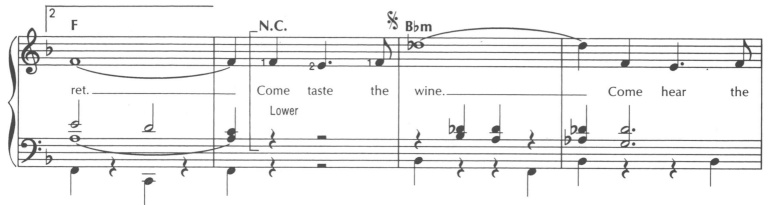

ret. Come taste the wine. Come hear the
Lower

band. Come blow the horn, start cel - e - brat - ing.

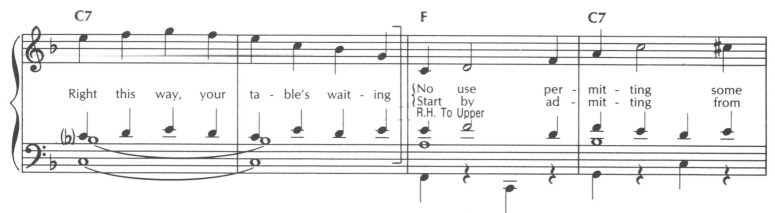

Right this way, your ta - ble's wait - ing {No use per - mit - ting some
Start by ad - mit - ting some from
R.H. To Upper

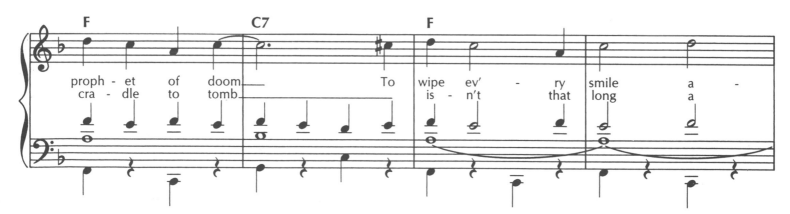

proph - et of doom To wipe ev' - ry smile a -
cra - dle to tomb is - n't that long a

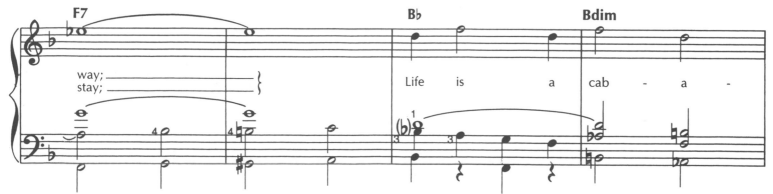

way; Life is a cab - a -
stay;

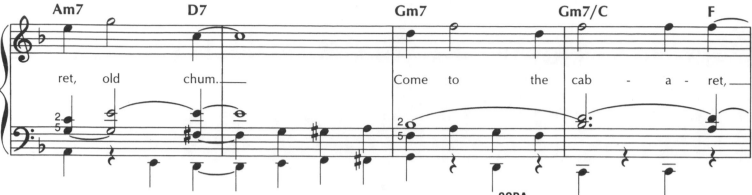

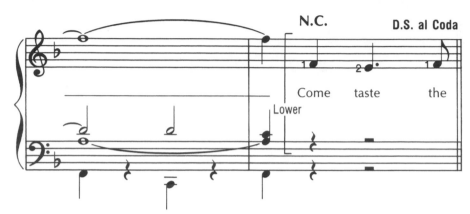

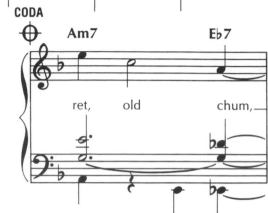

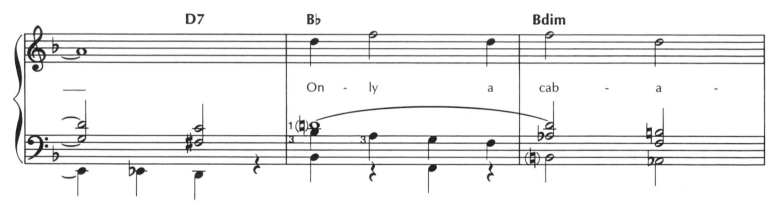

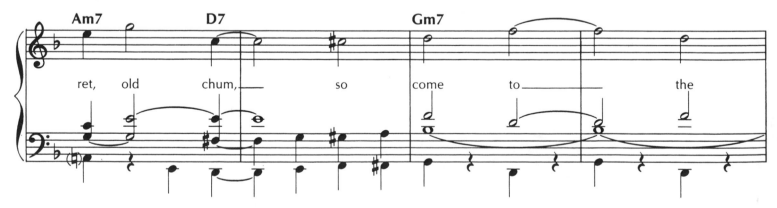

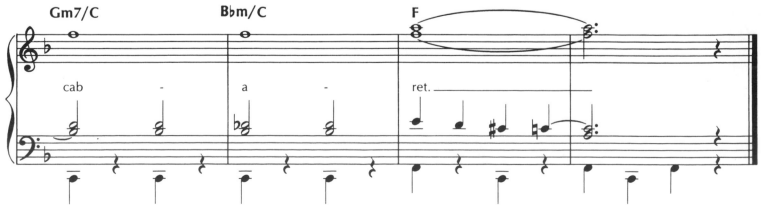

Do-Re-Mi

from THE SOUND OF MUSIC

Electronic Organs
Upper: Flutes (or Tibias) 16', 4', 2'
        Add Piano
Lower: Flute 8', 4', Strings 8',
Pedal: 16', 8', Sustain
Vib./Trem.: On, Full

Drawbar Organs
Upper: 70 0860 000
Lower: (00) 8654 110
Pedal: 68, Sustain
Vib./Trem.: On, Full

Lyrics by Oscar Hammerstein II
Music by Richard Rodgers

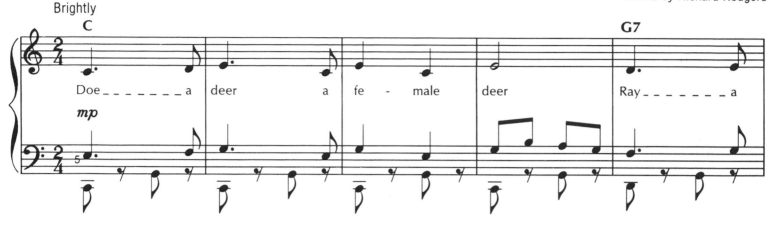

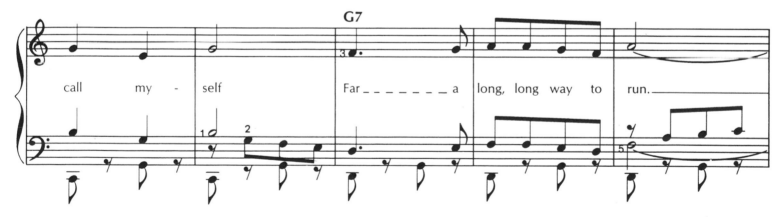

14

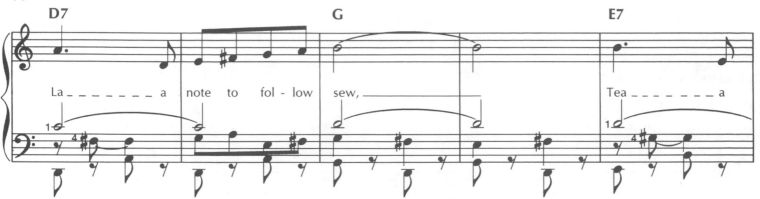

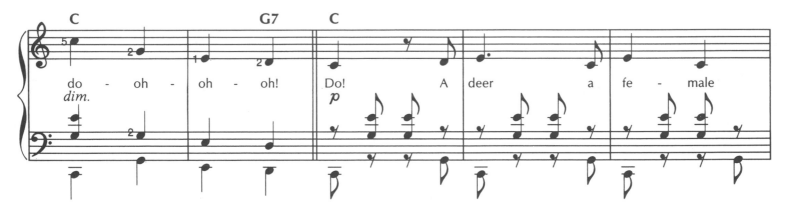

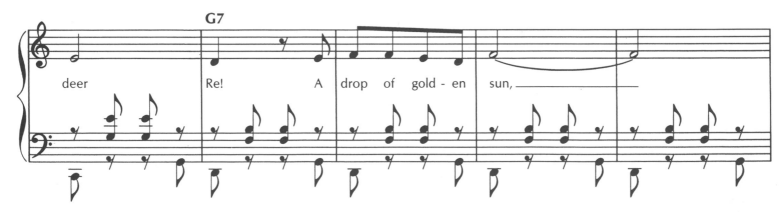

15

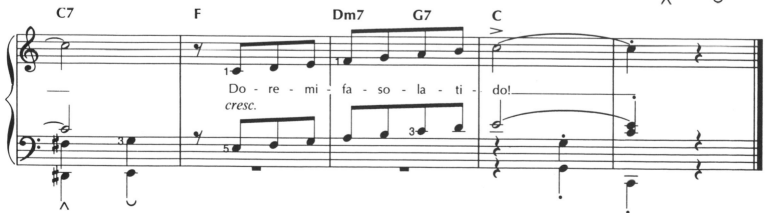

Climb Ev'ry Mountain

from THE SOUND OF MUSIC

Electronic Organs

Upper: Flutes (or Tibias) 16', 8', 2'
        Diapason 8', String 8'
Lower: Flutes 8', 4', String 8'
Pedal: Bourdon 16', String Bass
Vib./Trem.: On, Slow

Tonebar Organs

Upper: 80 8868 550
Lower: (00) 7704 000
Pedal: 64
Vib./Trem.: On, Slow

Lyrics by Oscar Hammerstein II
Music by Richard Rodgers

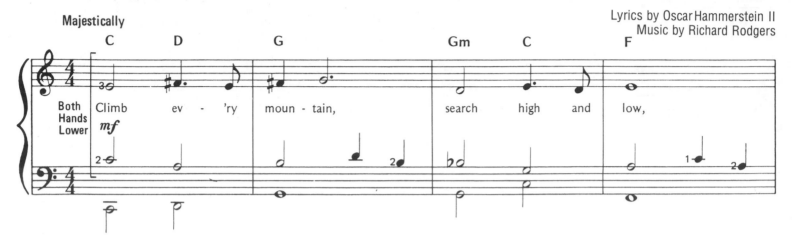

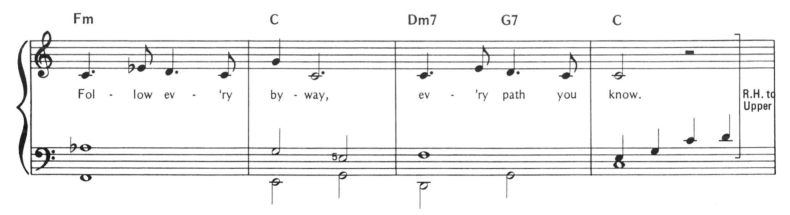

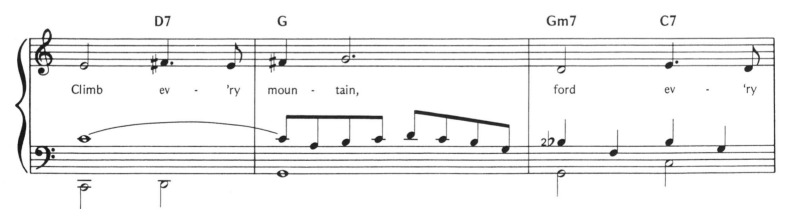

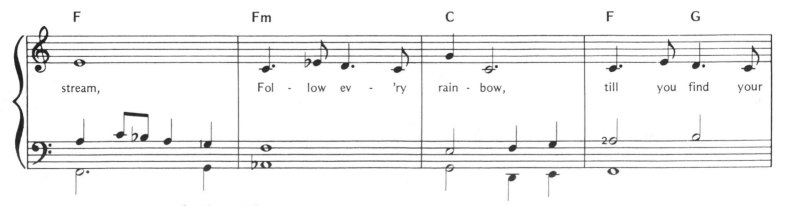

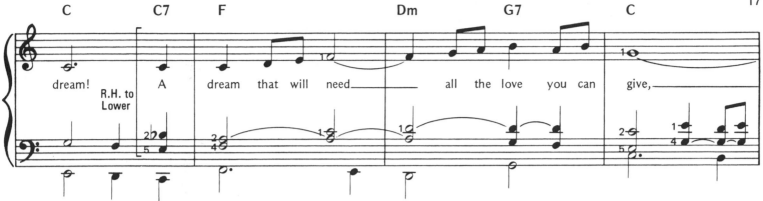

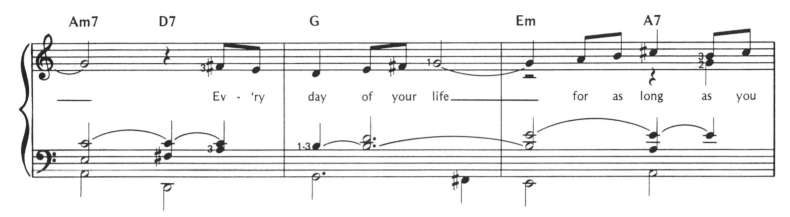

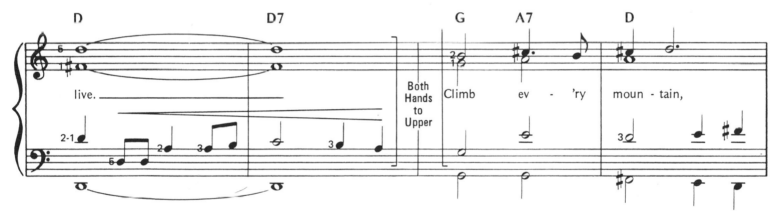

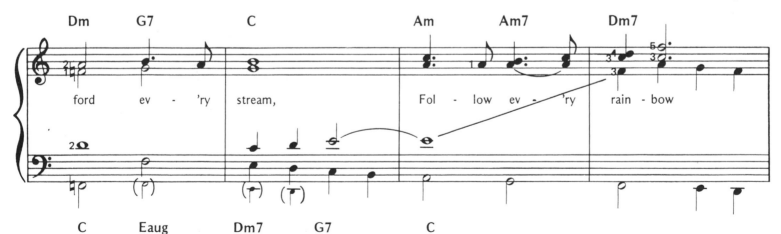

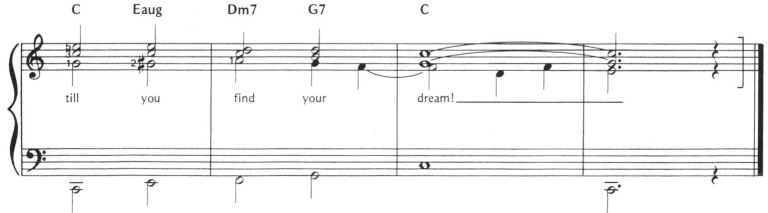

Day by Day
from the Musical GODSPELL

Electronic Organs
Upper: Flutes (or Tibias) 8', 4', 2⅓'
      String 4'
Lower: Flute 8', Strings 8', 4'
Pedal: 16', 8', Sustain
Vib./Trem.: On, Full

Drawbar Organs
Upper: 00 8800 850
Lower: (00) 8542 220
Pedal: 58, Sustain
Vib./Trem.: On, Full

Words and Music by
Stephen Schwartz

Moderate Waltz

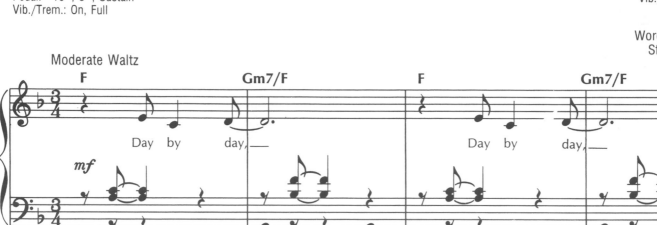

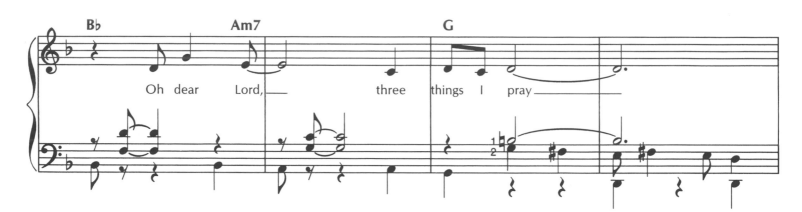

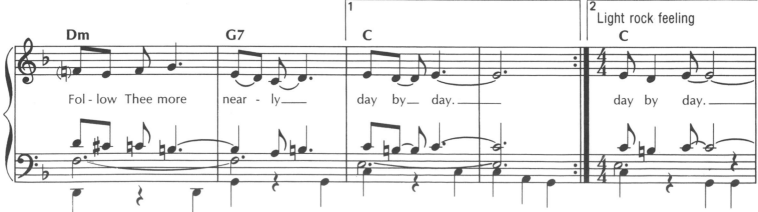

Edelweiss
from THE SOUND OF MUSIC

Electronic Organs

Upper: Flutes (or Tibias) 8', 2'
Lower: Flutes 8', 4'
Pedal: 16', 8'
Vib./Trem.: On, Slow

Tonebar Organs

Upper: 00 7004 000
Lower: (00) 5300 000
Pedal: 24
Vib./Trem.: On, Slow

Lyrics by Oscar Hammerstein II
Music by Richard Rodgers

Slowly, with expression

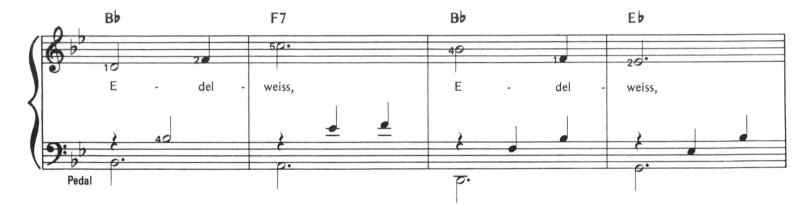

E - del - weiss, E - del - weiss,

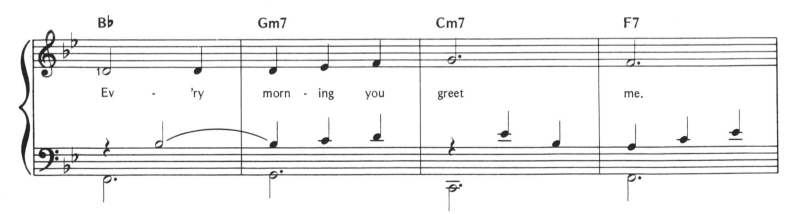

Ev - 'ry morn - ing you greet me.

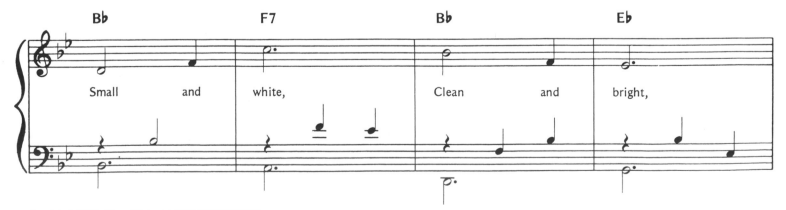

Small and white, Clean and bright,

21

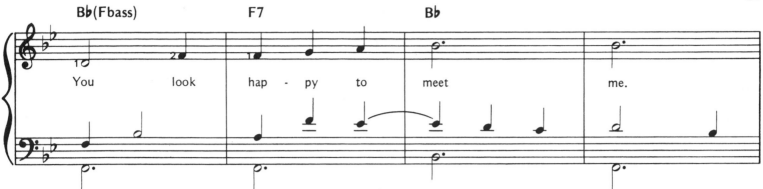

You look hap - py to meet me.

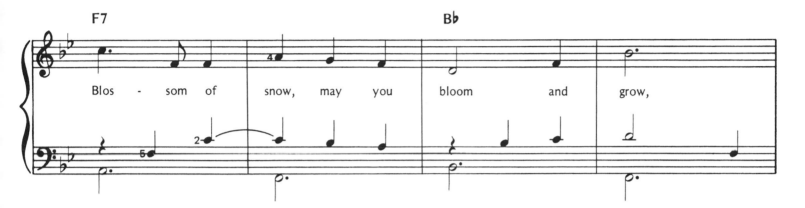

Blos - som of snow, may you bloom and grow,

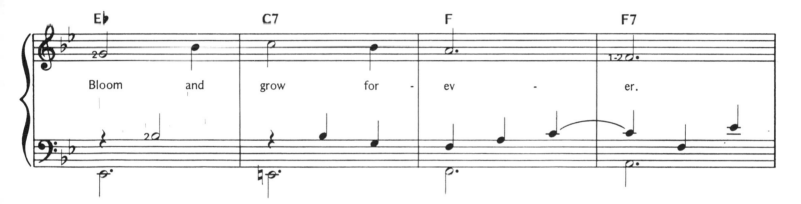

Bloom and grow for - ev - er.

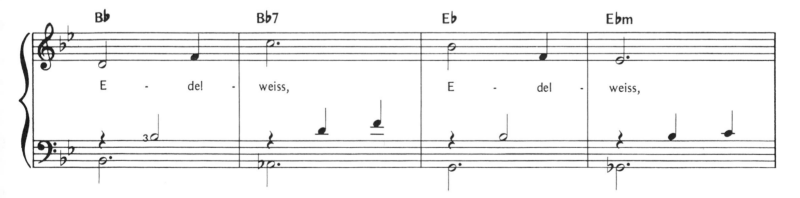

E - del - weiss, E - del - weiss,

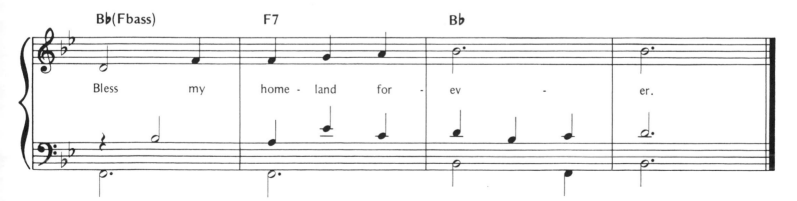

Bless my home - land for - ev - er.

Everything's Coming Up Roses

from GYPSY

Electronic Organs

Upper: Flutes (or Tibias) 8', 4'
      String 8'
Lower: Diapason 8', Flute 8'
Pedal: 16', 8', Sustain
Vib./Trem.: On, Full

Drawbar Organs

Upper: 00 8656 446
Lower: (00) 8643 444
Pedal: 68, Sustain
Vib./Trem.: On, Full

Words by Stephen Sondheim
Music by Jule Styne

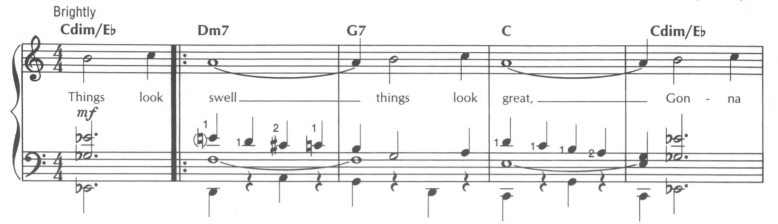

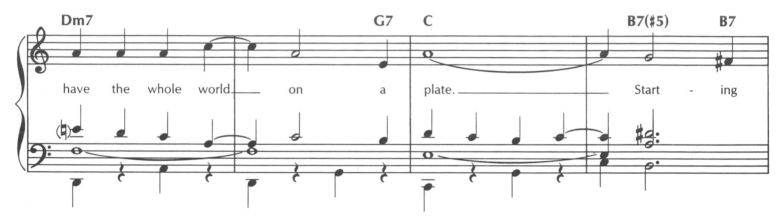

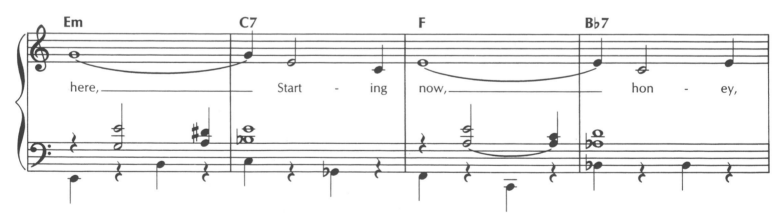

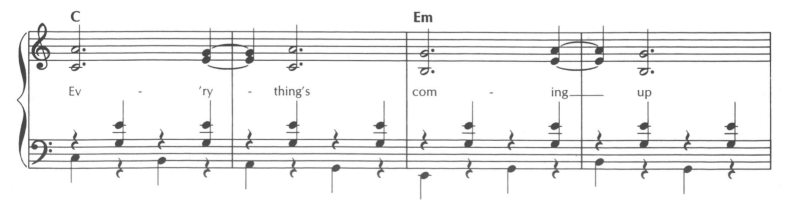

23

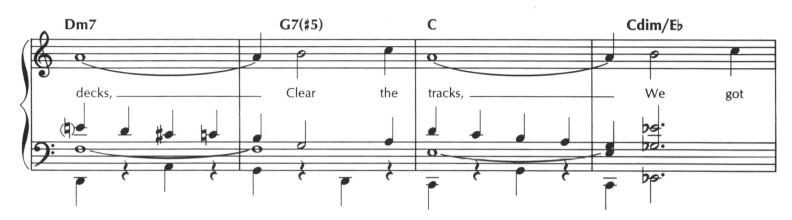

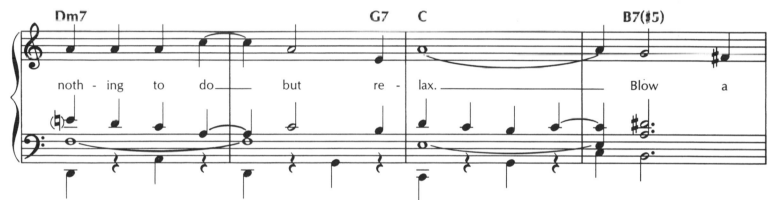

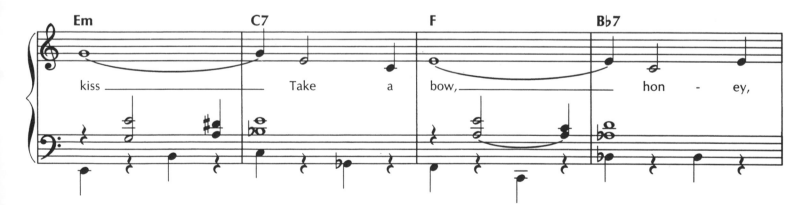

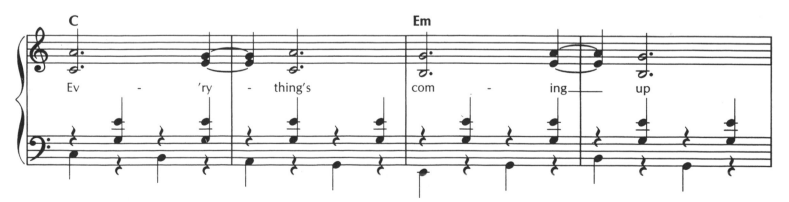

24

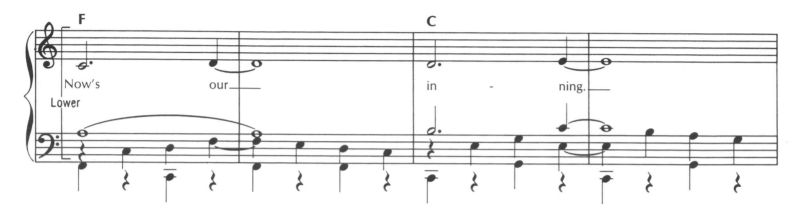

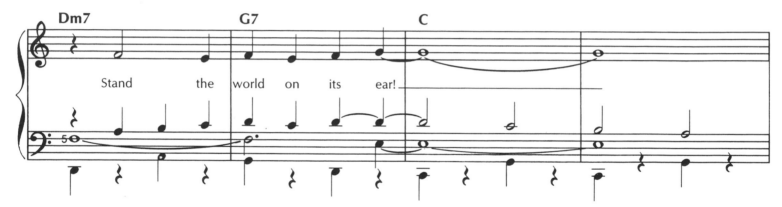

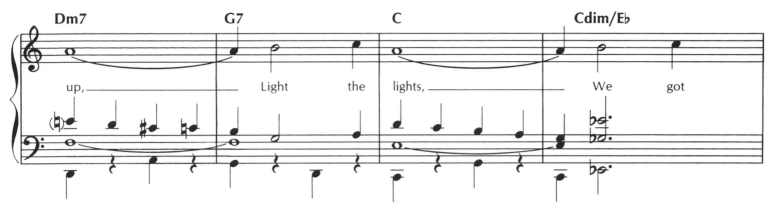

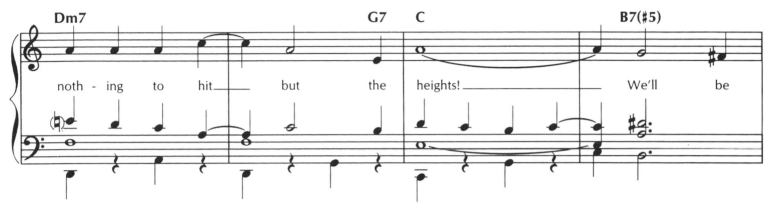

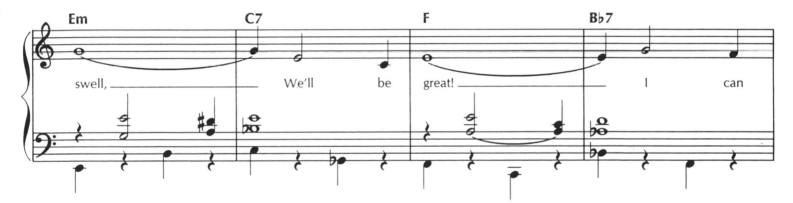

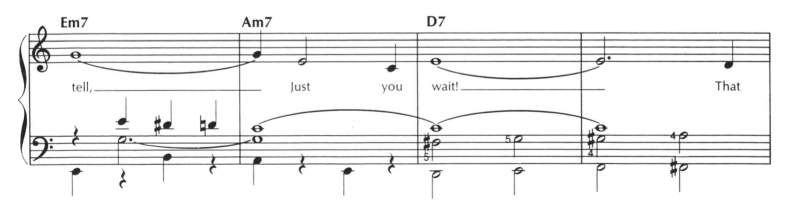

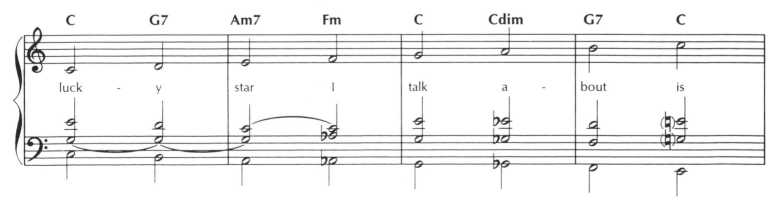

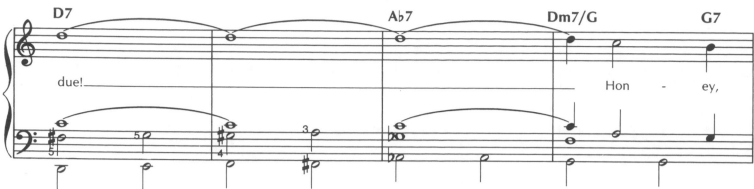

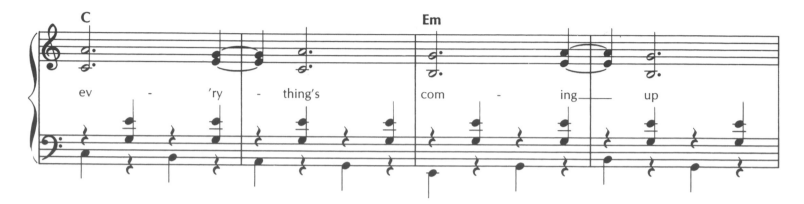

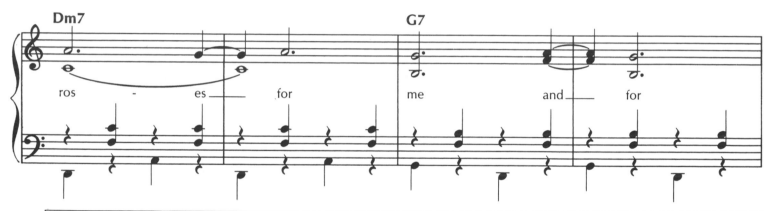

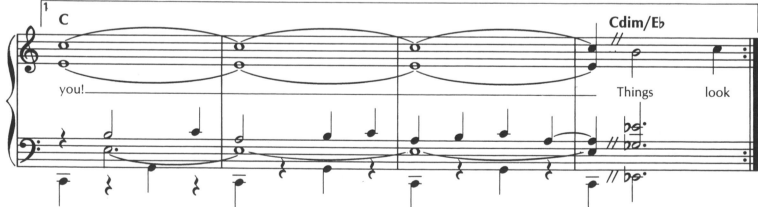

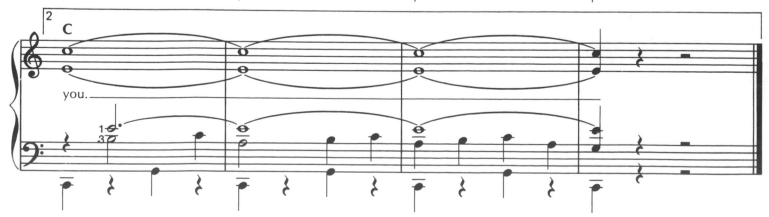

Get Me to the Church on Time

from MY FAIR LADY

Electronic Organs

Upper: Flutes (or Tibias) 16′, 8′, 2′
       Trumpet
Lower: Flute 4′, Diapason 8′,
       Reed 8′
Pedal: String Bass
Vib./Trem.: On, Fast

Tonebar Organs

Upper: 80 6368 006
Lower: (00) 8365 002
Pedal: String Bass
Vib./Trem.: On, Fast

Words by Alan Jay Lerner
Music by Frederick Loewe

Brightly

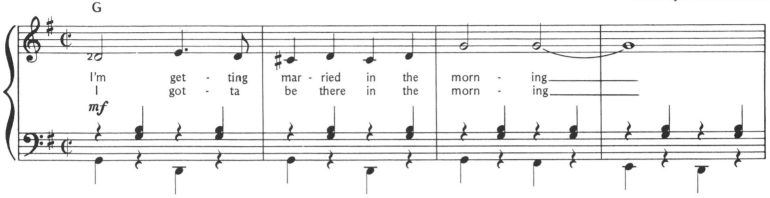

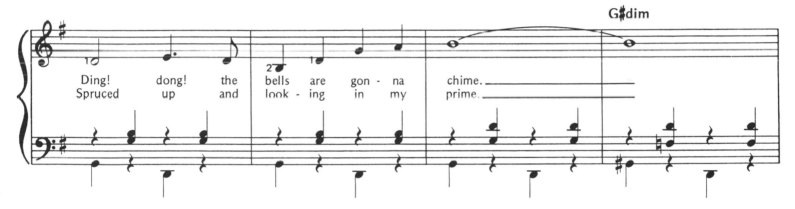

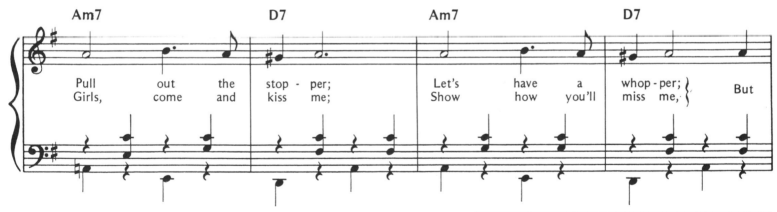

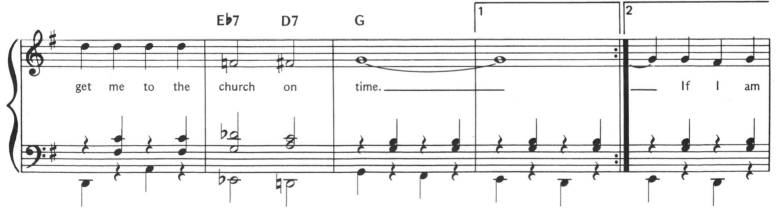

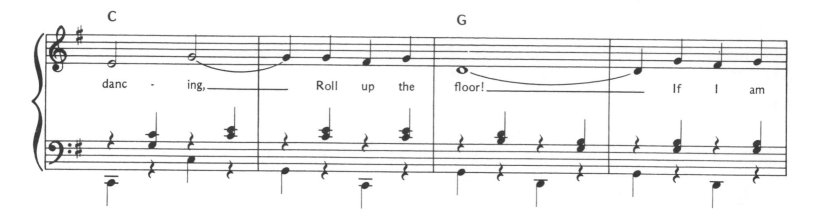

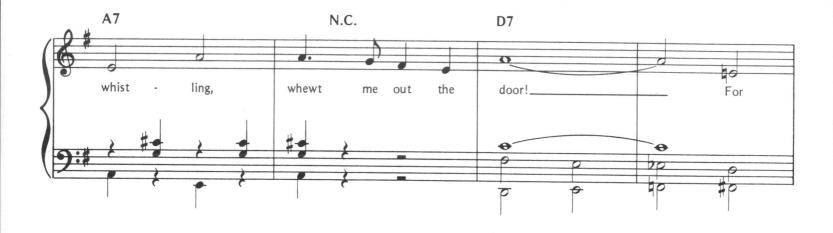

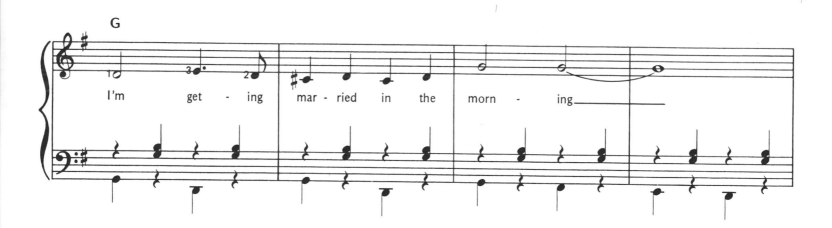

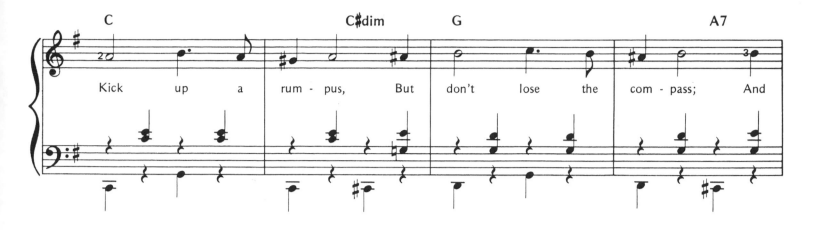

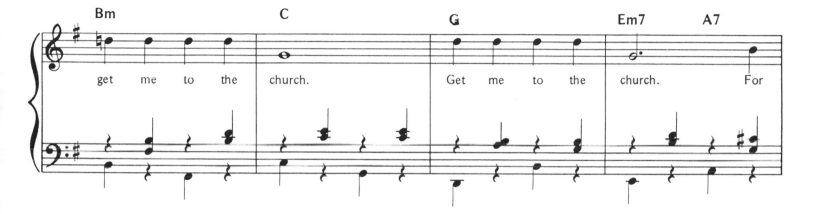

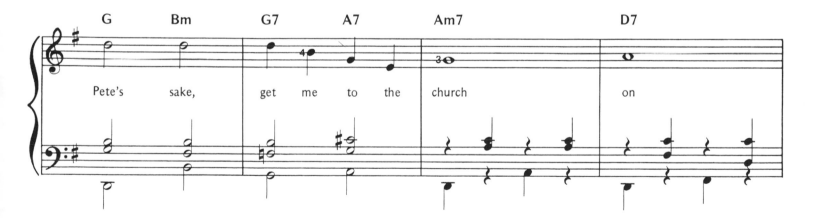

Hello, Young Lovers
from THE KING AND I

Electronic Organs

Upper: String 8′, Flute (or Tibia) 8′
Lower: Flutes 8′, 4′
Pedal: 16′, 8′
Vib./Trem.: On, Slow

Tonebar Organs

Upper: 00 5233 210
Lower: (00) 4300 000
Pedal: 23
Vib./Trem.: On, Slow

Lyrics by Oscar Hammerstein II
Music by Richard Rodgers

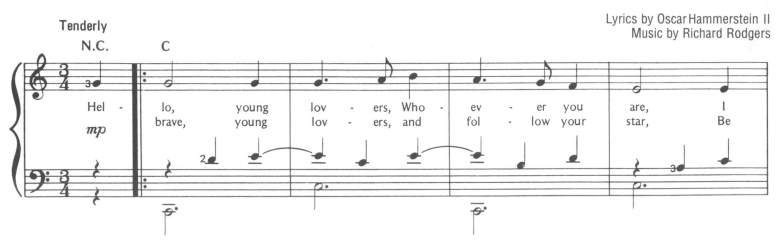

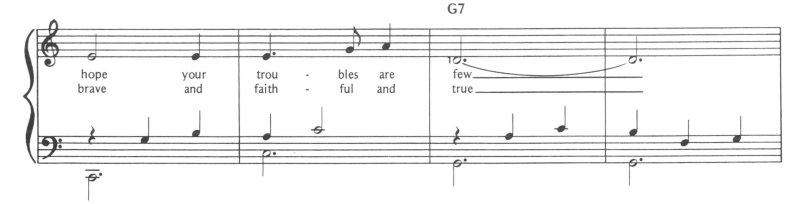

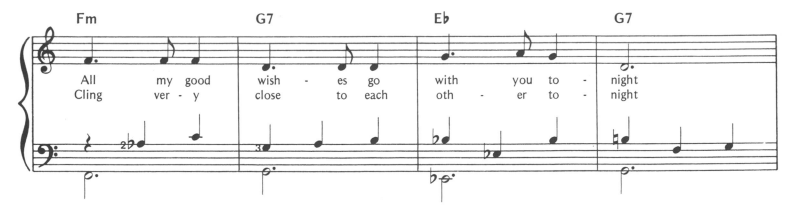

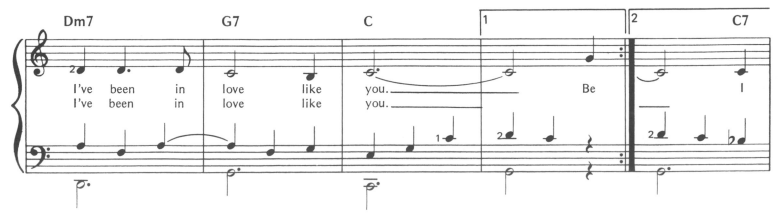

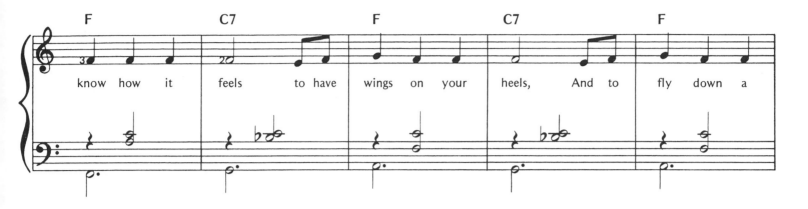

know how it feels to have wings on your heels, And to fly down a

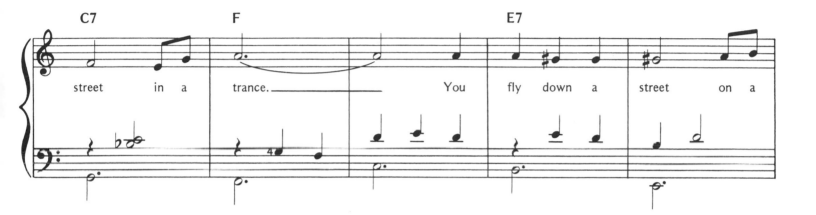

street in a trance. You fly down a street on a

chance that you'll meet, And you meet not real - ly by chance.

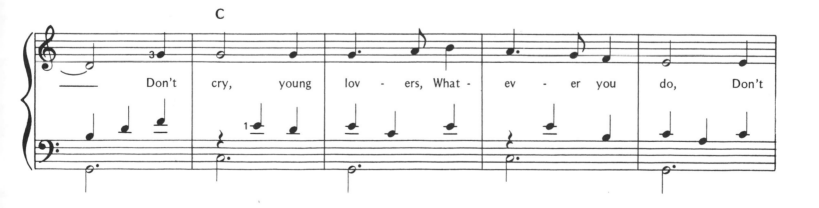

Don't cry, young lov - ers, What - ev - er you do, Don't

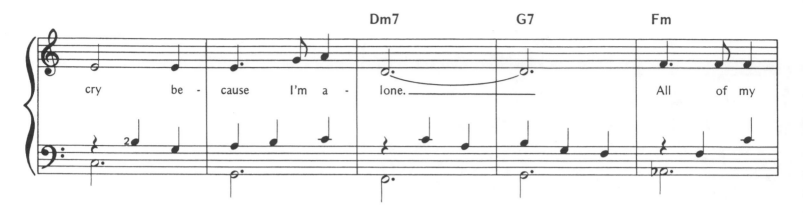

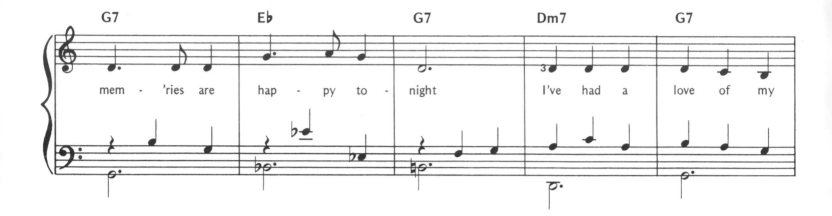

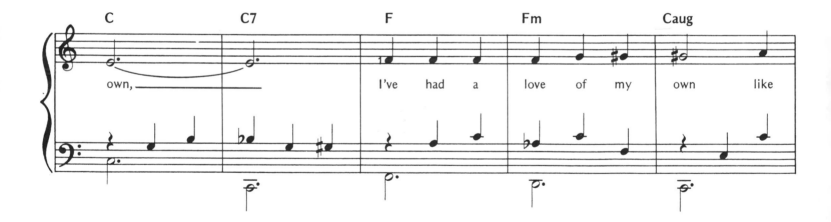

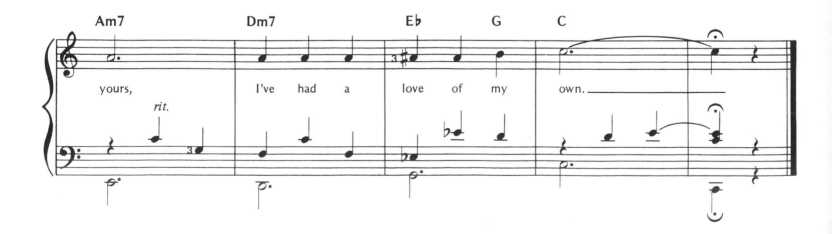

How Are Things in Glocca Morra

from FINIAN'S RAINBOW

Electronic Organs
Upper: Flute (or Tibia) 4', Reed 8'
Lower: Flutes 8', 4', String 8'
Pedal: 16', 8', Sustain
Vib./Trem.: Upper-Off
Lower-On, Full

Drawbar Organs
Upper: 00 4880 000
Lower: (00) 8542 200
Pedal: 68, Sustain
Vib./Trem.: Upper-Off
Lower-On, Full

Words by E.Y. Harburg
Music by Burton Lane

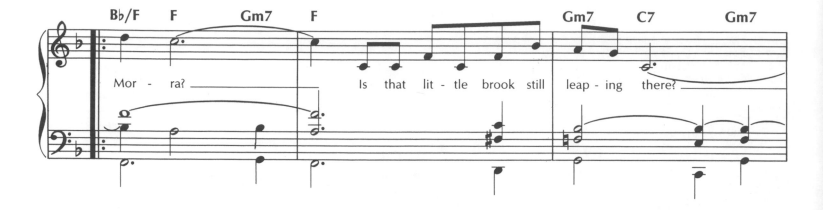

Mor - ra? _____ Is that lit - tle brook still leap - ing there? _____

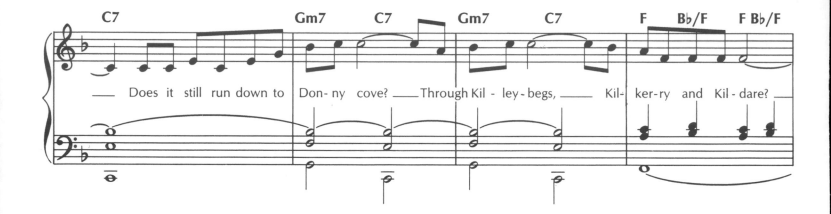

_____ Does it still run down to Don- ny cove? _____ Through Kil - ley - begs, _____ Kil- ker - ry and Kil - dare? _____

(with a steady beat)

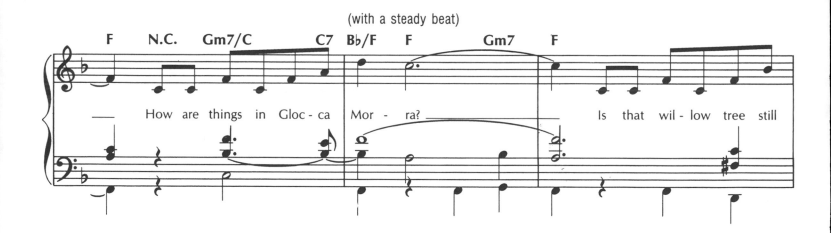

_____ How are things in Gloc - ca Mor - ra? _____ Is that wil - low tree still

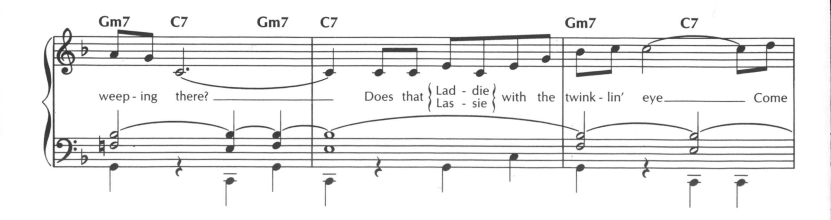

weep - ing there? _____ Does that {Lad - die / Las - sie} with the twink - lin' eye _____ Come

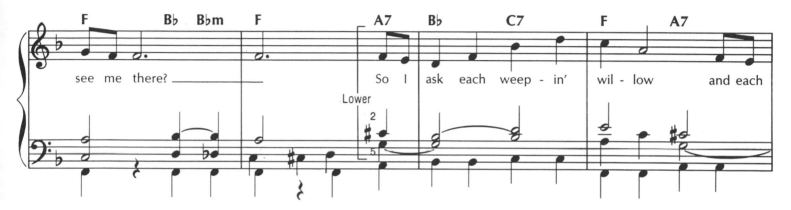

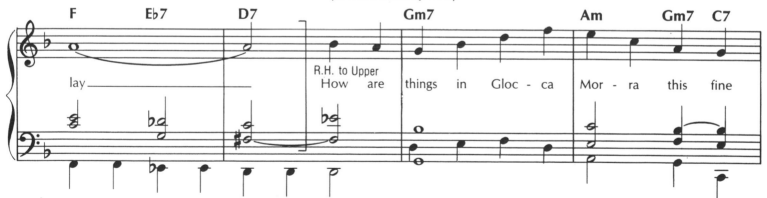

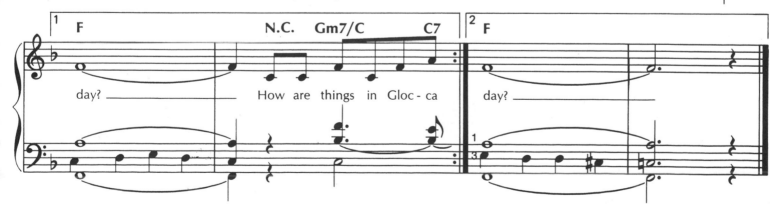

I Could Have Danced All Night

from MY FAIR LADY

Electronic Organs

Upper: Flutes (or Tibias) 16', 8'
       String 4'
Lower: Flute 8', Diapason 8',
       String 8'
Pedal: 16', 8'
Vib./Trem.: On, Fast

Tonebar Organs

Upper: 81 5505 004
Lower: (00) 7343 312
Pedal: 45
Vib./Trem.: On, Fast

Words by Alan Jay Lerner
Music by Frederick Loewe

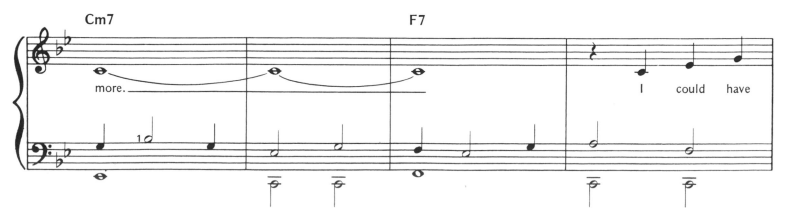

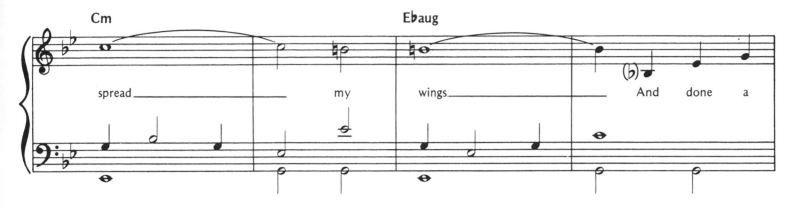

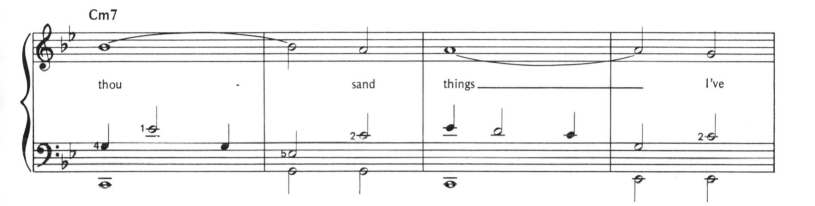

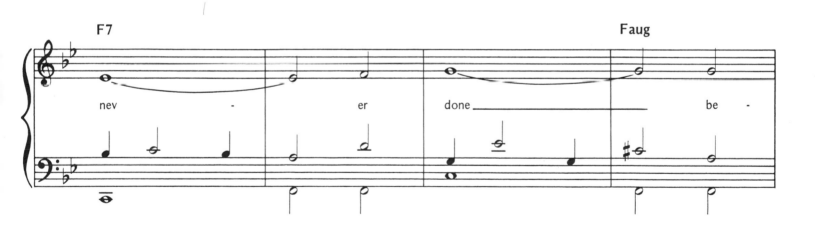

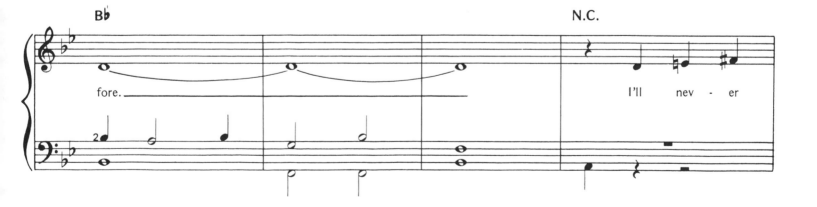

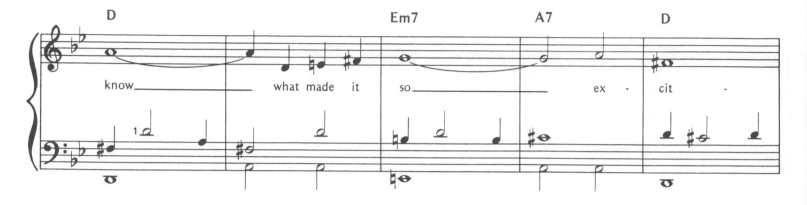

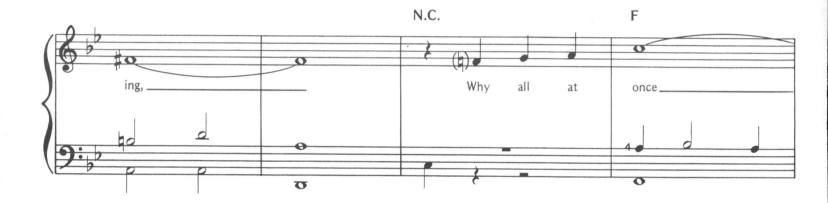

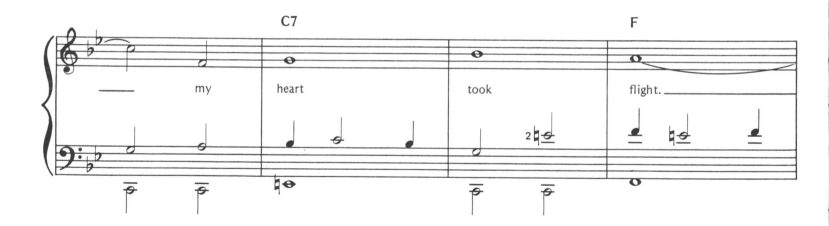

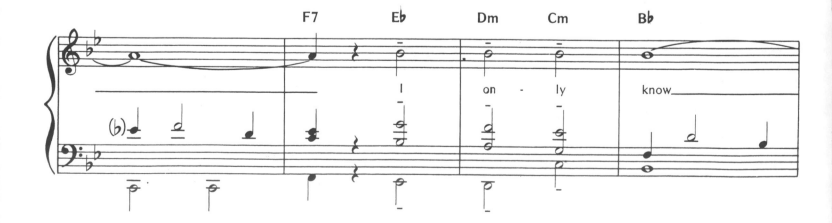

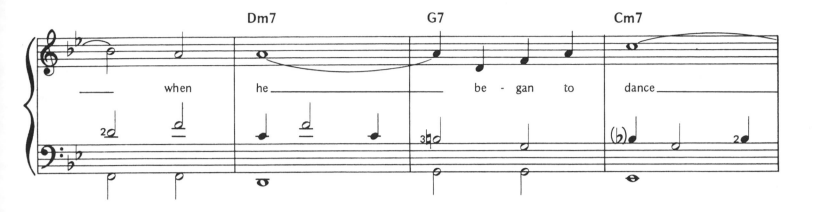

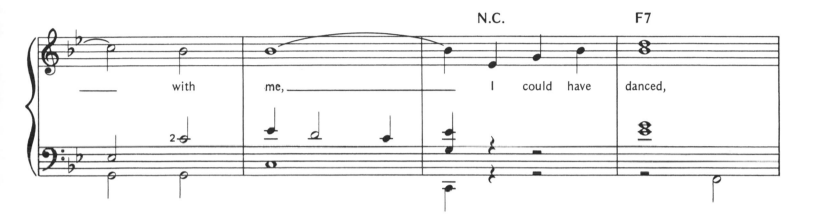

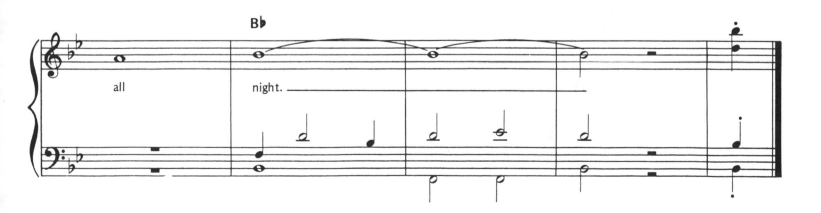

I Loved You Once in Silence

from CAMELOT

Electronic Organs

Upper: Flutes (or Tibias) 8′, 4′
        Reed 8′
Lower: Flute 8′, Diapason 8′
Pedal: 16′, 8′
Vib./Trem.: On, Slow

Tonebar Organs

Upper: 00 8525 322
Lower: (00) 6311 000
Pedal: 45 .
Vib./Trem.: On, Slow

Words by Alan Jay Lerner
Music by Frederick Loewe

With simple expression

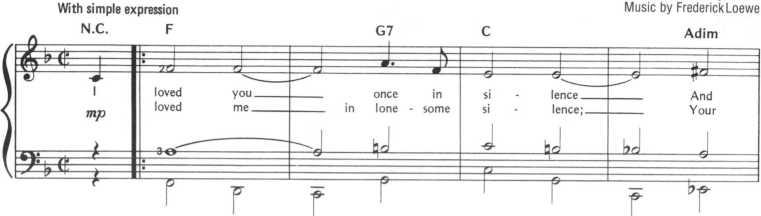

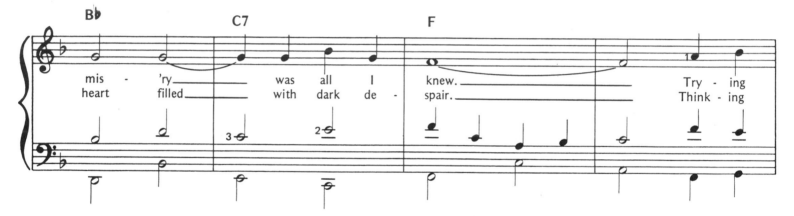

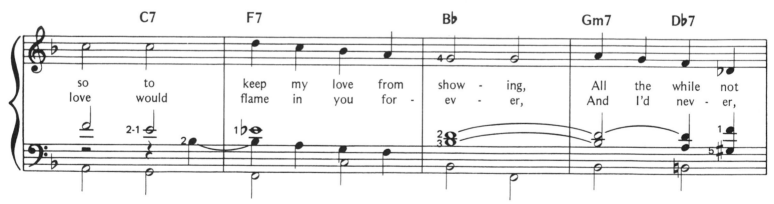

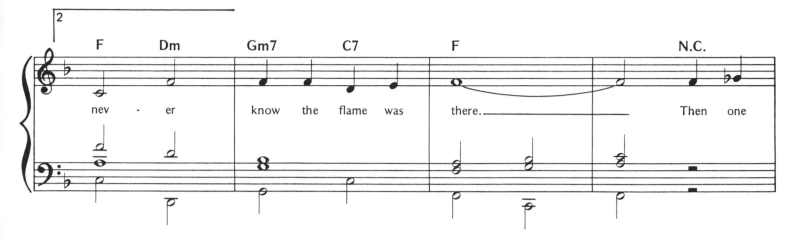

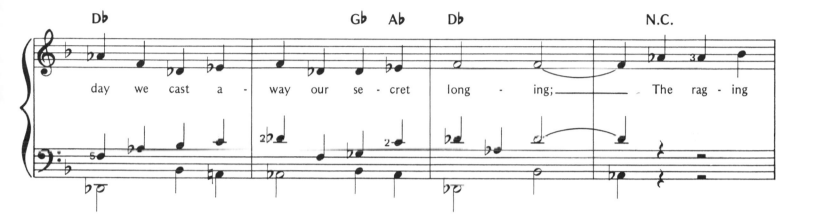

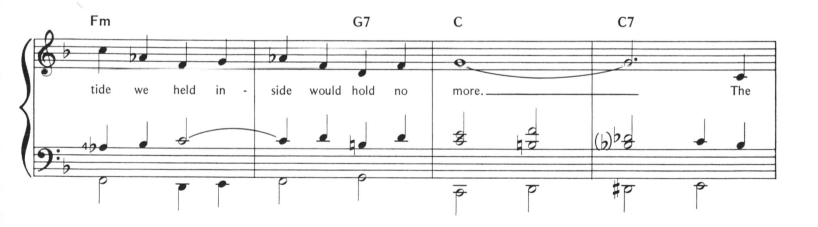

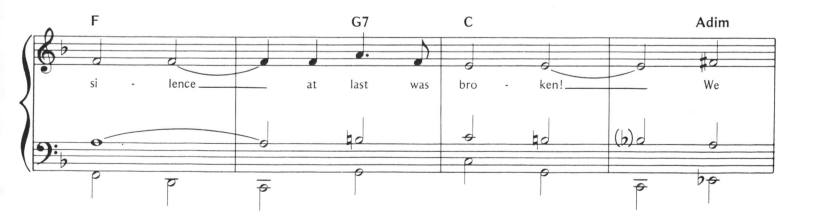

42

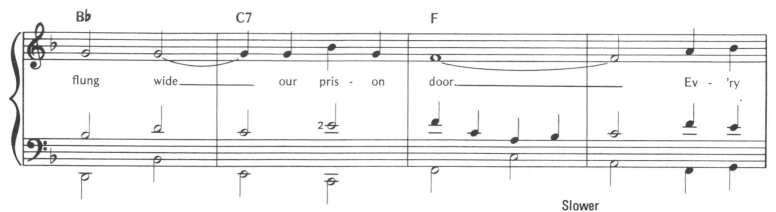

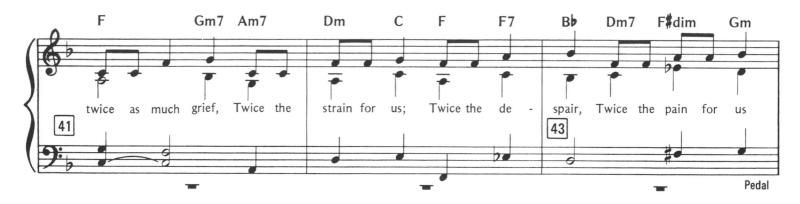

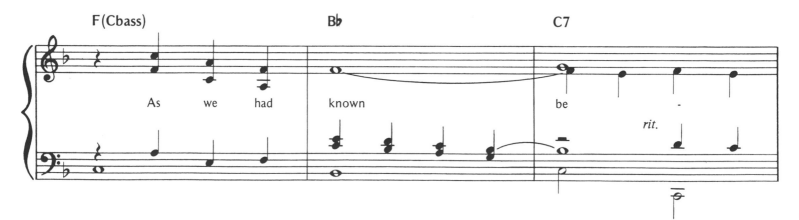

I Still See Elisa

from PAINT YOUR WAGON

Electronic Organs

Upper: Flutes (or Tibias) 16′, 8′,
        String 4′
Lower: Flute 8′, Diapason 8′,
        String 8′
Pedal: 16′, 8′
Vib./Trem.: On, Fast

Tonebar Organs

Upper: 81 5505 004
Lower: (00) 7343 312
Pedal: 44
Vib./Trem.: On, Fast

Words by Alan Jay Lerner
Music by Frederick Loewe

Slowly

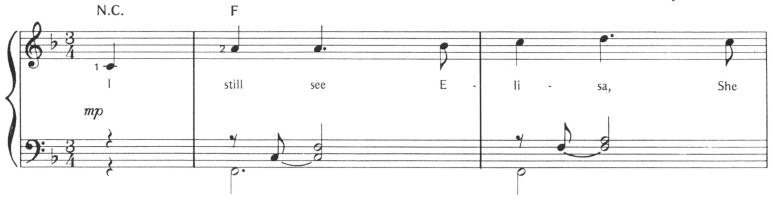

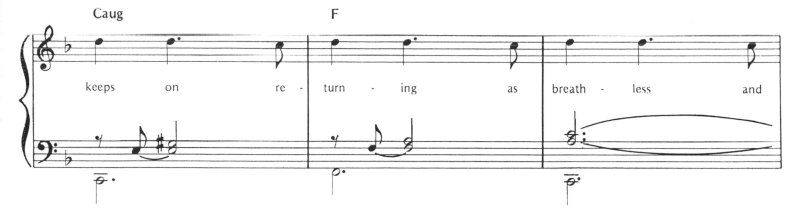

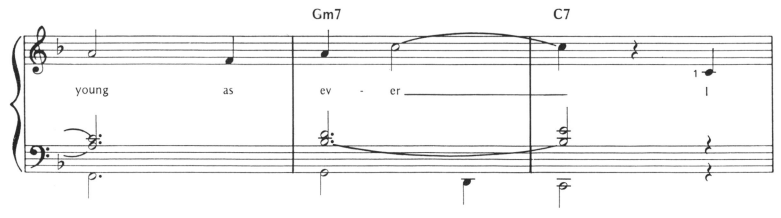

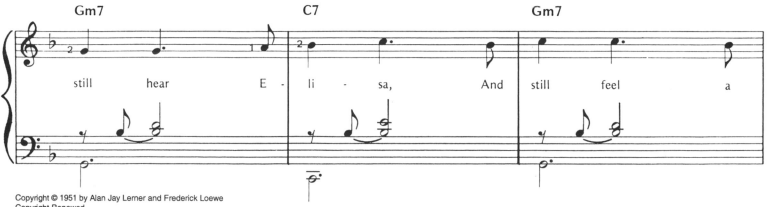

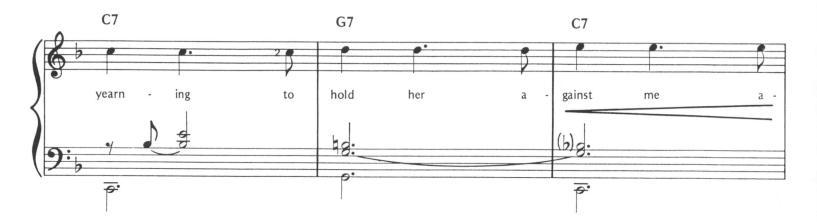

yearn - ing to hold her a - gainst me a -

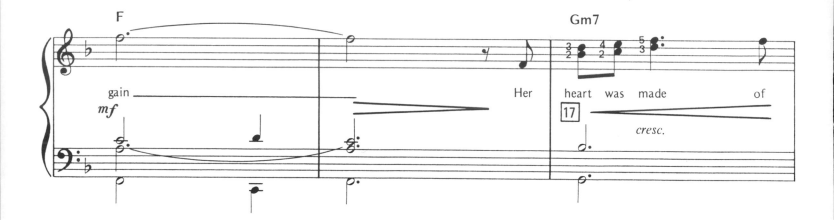

gain *mf* Her heart was made of
cresc.

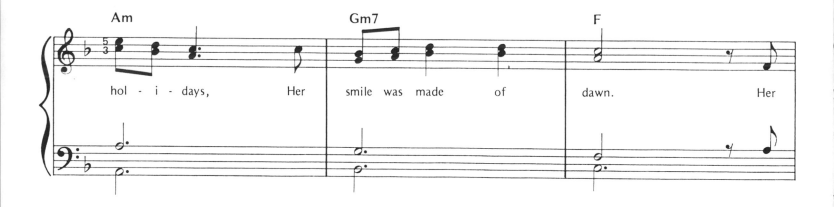

hol - i - days, Her smile was made of dawn. Her

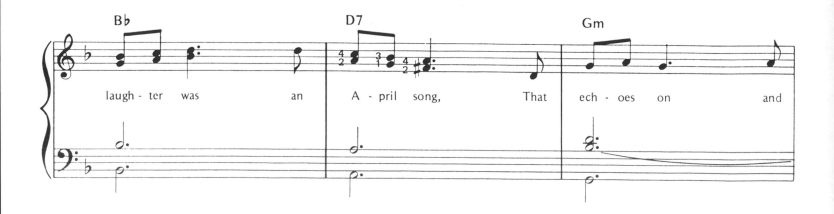

laugh - ter was an A - pril song, That ech - oes on and

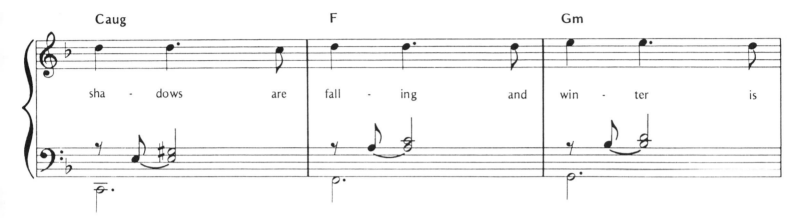

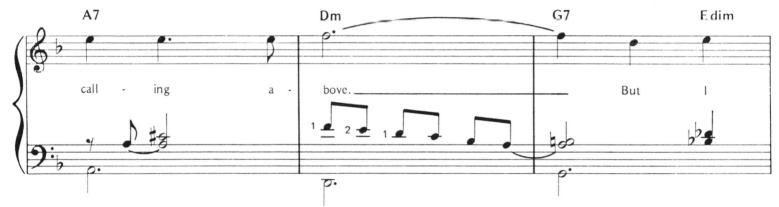

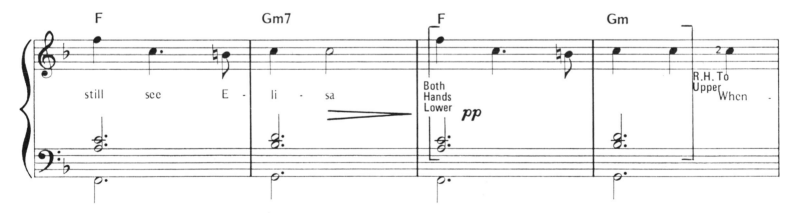

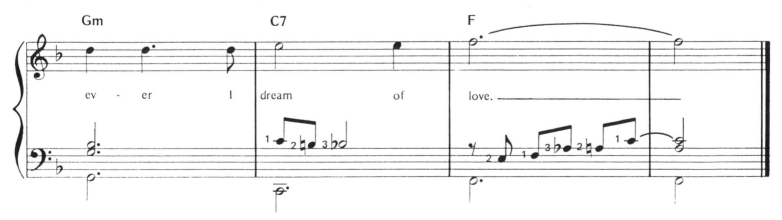

I Whistle a Happy Tune

from THE KING AND I

Electronic Organs

Upper: Flutes (or Tibias) 8', 2⅔', 2'
       Reed 4'
Lower: Flutes 8', 4', String 8'
Pedal: 16', 8', Sustain
Vib./Trem.: On, Full

Drawbar Organs

Upper: 00 8088 000
Lower: (00) 8533 200
Pedal: 68, Sustain
Vib./Trem.: On, Full

Lyrics by Oscar Hammerstein II
Music by Richard Rodgers

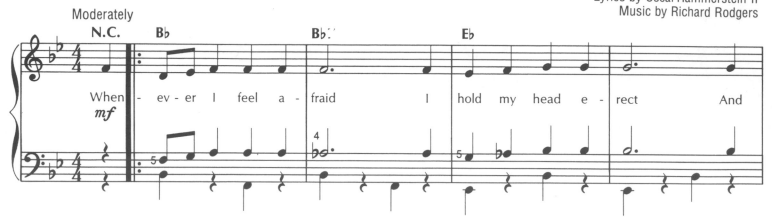

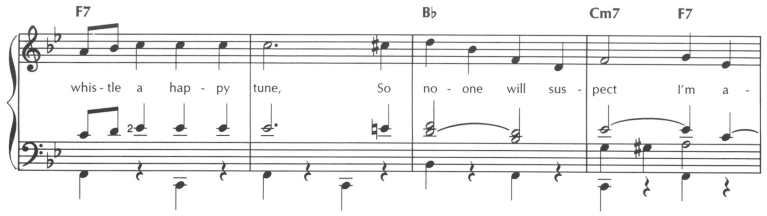

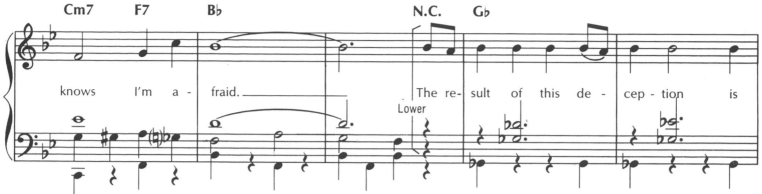

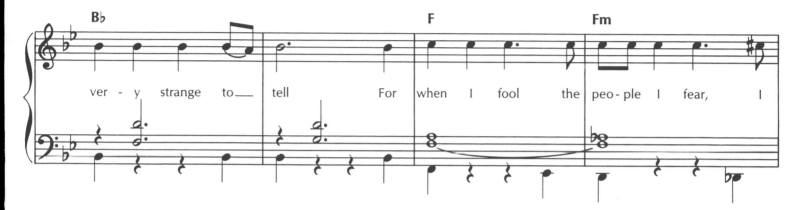

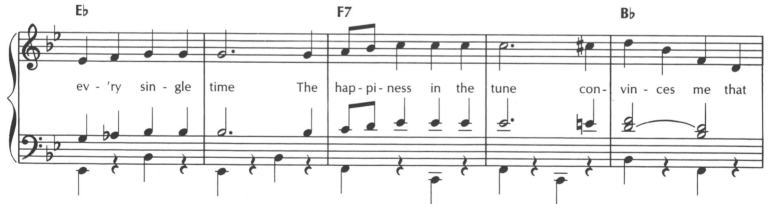

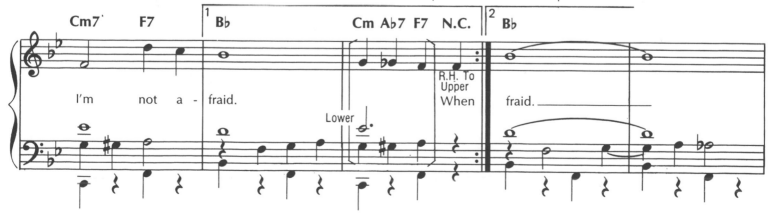

Make be - lieve you're brave and the trick will take you far.

Lower

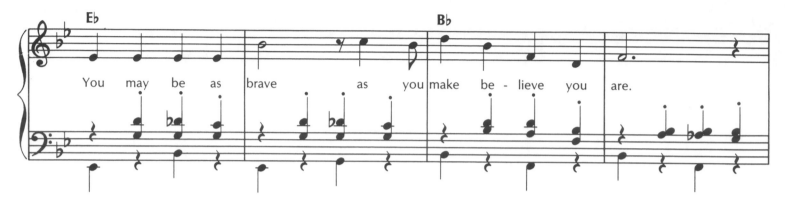

You may be as brave as you make be - lieve you are.

8va

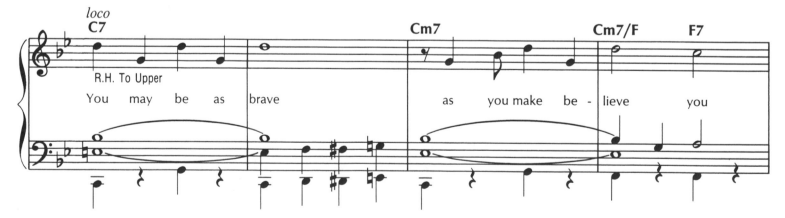

loco

R.H. To Upper

You may be as brave as you make be - lieve you

are.

It Might As Well Be Spring

from STATE FAIR

Electronic Organs

Upper: Flutes (or Tibias) 16', 4', 2'
Lower: Melodia 8'
Pedal: 8'
Vib./Trem.: On, Slow

Tonebar Organs

Upper: 50 0402 002
Lower: (00) 4210 000
Pedal: 05
Vib./Trem.: On, Slow

Lyrics by Oscar Hammerstein II
Music by Richard Rodgers

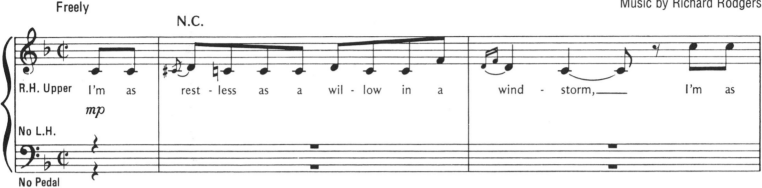

I'm as rest-less as a wil-low in a wind - storm, _____ I'm as

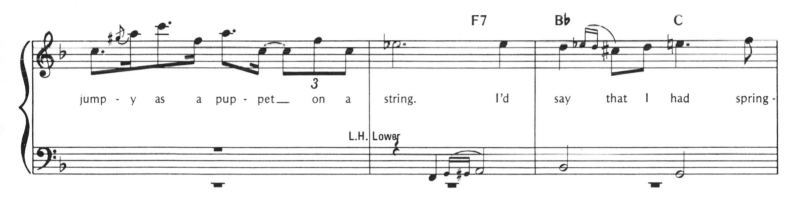

jump - y as a pup-pet __ on a string. I'd say that I had spring-

fe - ver, But I know it is - n't spring. I am

star - ry eyed and vague -ly dis-con - tent-ed, Like a night-in-gale with-out a song to

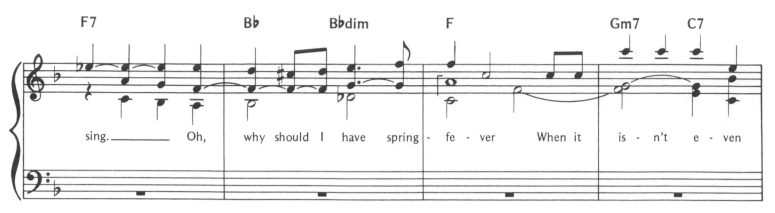

sing. _____ Oh, why should I have spring - fe - ver When it is - n't e - ven

spring? I keep wish - ing I were some-where else, Walk- ing down a strange new

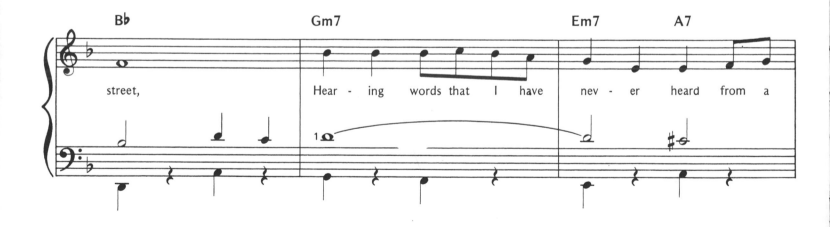

street, Hear - ing words that I have nev - er heard from a

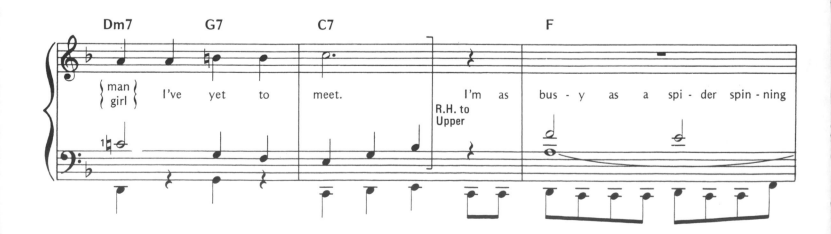

man / girl I've yet to meet. I'm as bus - y as a spi - der spin - ning

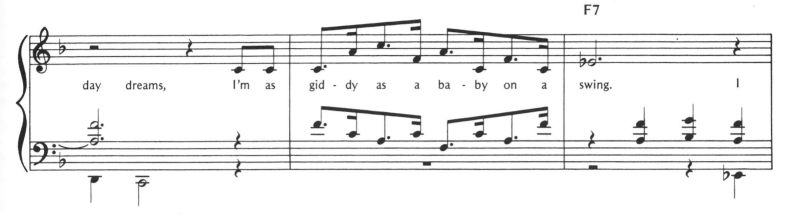

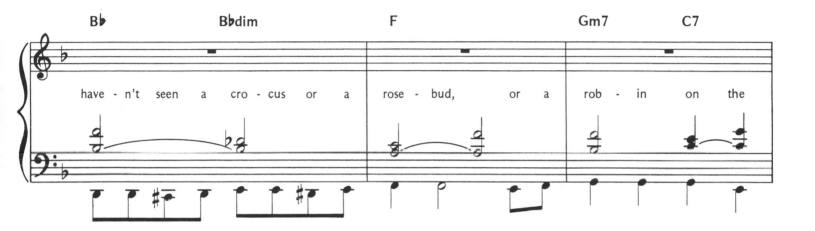

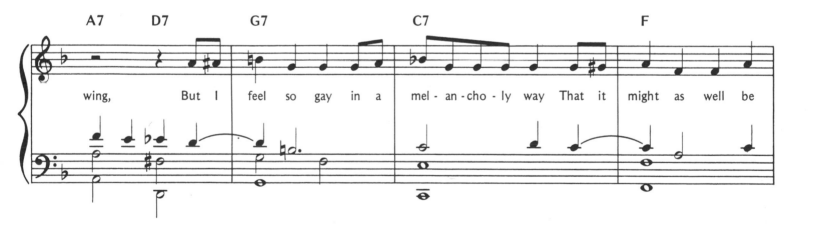

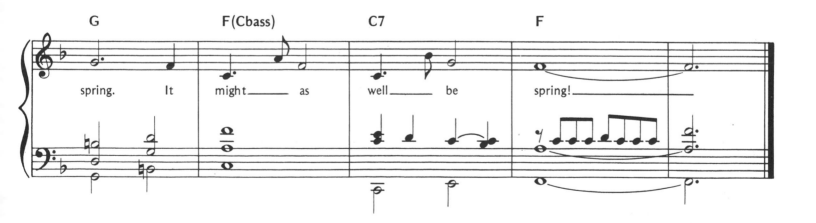

Just in Time

from BELLS ARE RINGING

Electronic Organs

Upper: Clarinet 8'
Lower: Flutes (or Tibias) 8', 4'
Pedal: 8'
Vib./Trem.: On, Slow, or Off

Tonebar Organs

Upper: 00 7050 000
Lower: (00) 5500 000
Pedal: 04
Vib./Trem.: On, Slow, or Off

Words by Betty Comden and Adolph Green
Music by Jule Styne

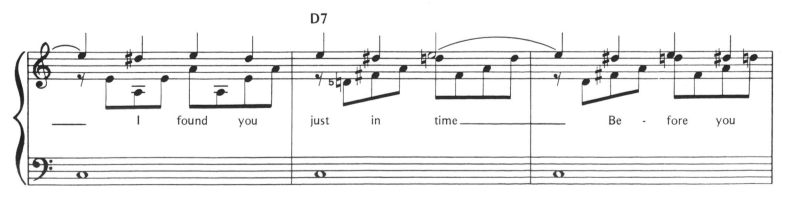

came, my time_____ was run - ing low._____

_____ I was lost,_____ The los - ing

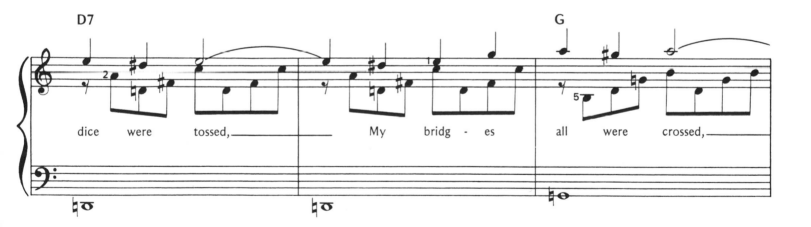

dice were tossed,_____ My bridg - es all were crossed,_____

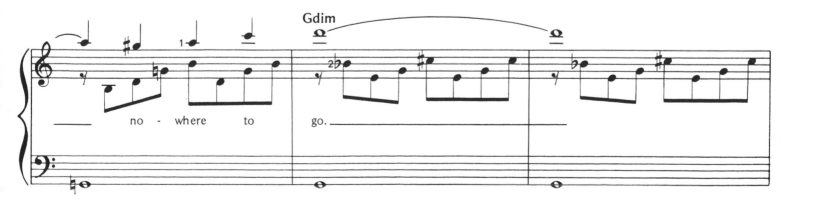

_____ no - where to go._____

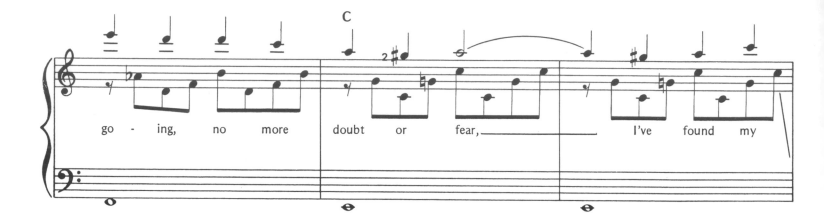

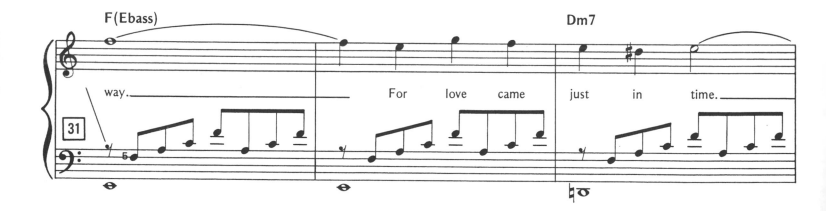

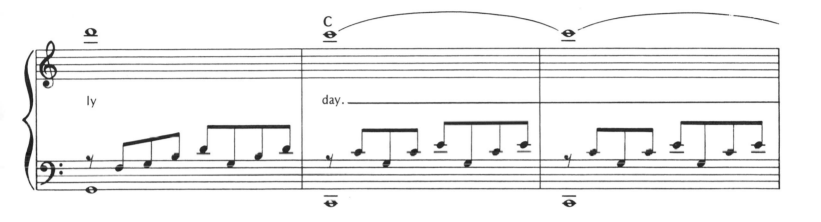

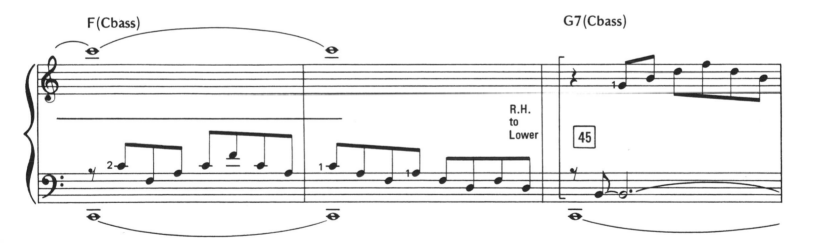

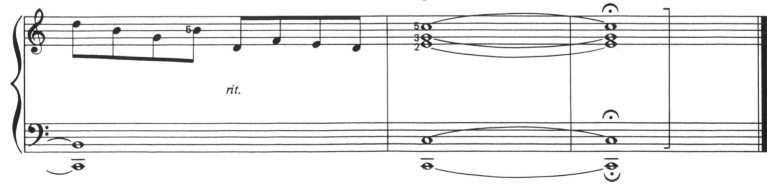

55

The Lady Is a Tramp

from BABES IN ARMS
from WORDS AND MUSIC

Electronic Organs

Upper: Flutes (or Tibias) 8′, 4′, 2⅔′, 2′
           Add Percuss
Lower: Flutes 8′, 4′
Pedal: String Bass
Vib./Trem.: On, Slow

Tonebar Organs

Upper: 00 8360 304
           Add Percuss
Lower: (00) 6402 003
Pedal: String Bass
Vib./Trem.: On, Slow

Words by Lorenz Hart
Music by Richard Rodgers

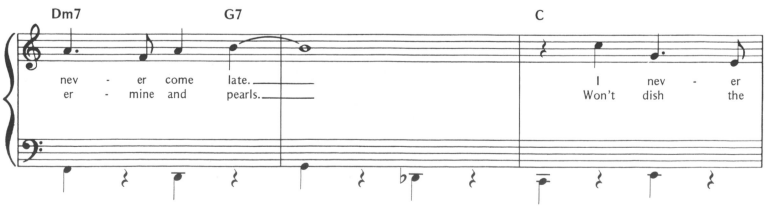

57

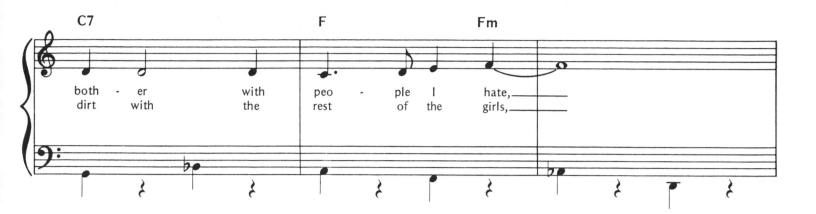

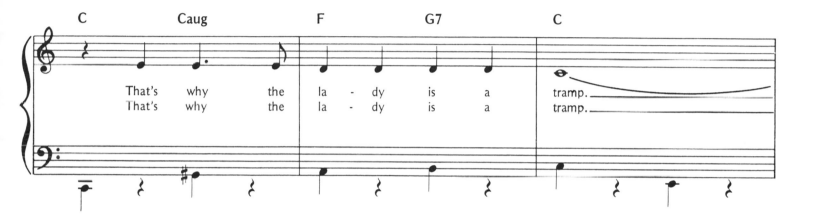

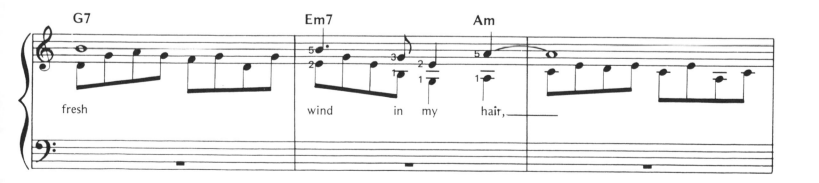

58

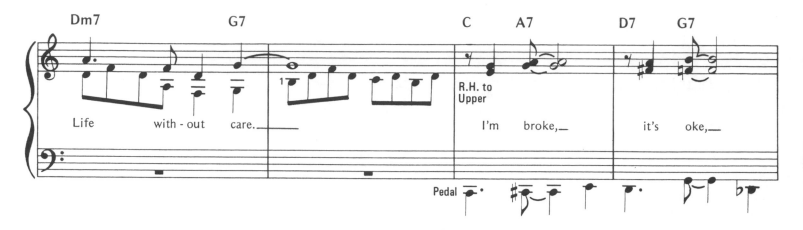

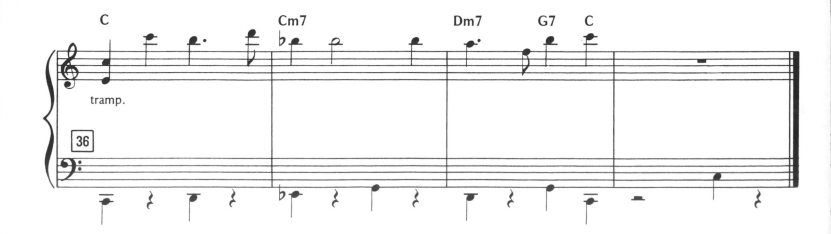

Mr. Wonderful
from the Musical MR. WONDERFUL

Electronic Organs
Upper: Flutes (or Tibias) 8', 4', 2⅔'
      Reed 8'
Lower: Flutes 8', 4', String 8'
Pedal: 16', 8', Sustain
Vib./Trem.: On, Full

Drawbar Organs
Upper: 00 8283 321
Lower: (00) 8654 210
Pedal: 66, Sustain
Vib./Trem.: On, Full

Words and Music by Jerry Bock,
Larry Holofcener and George David Weiss

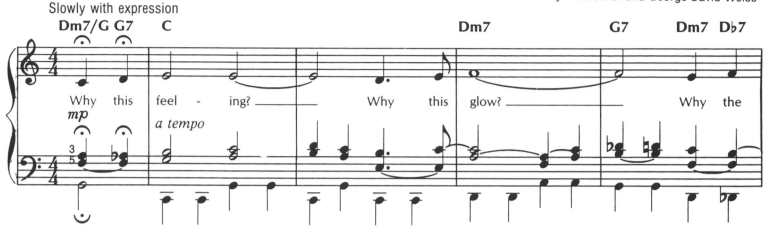

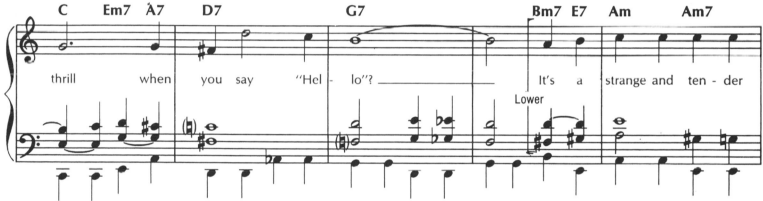

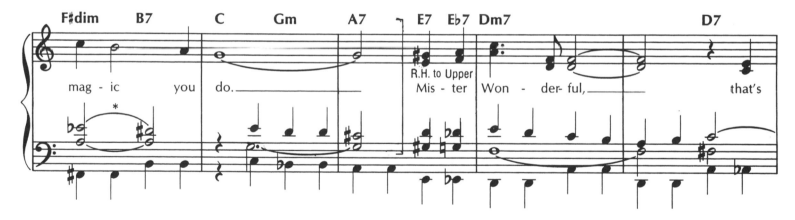

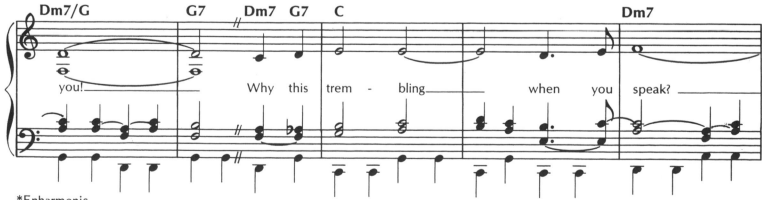

*Enharmonic

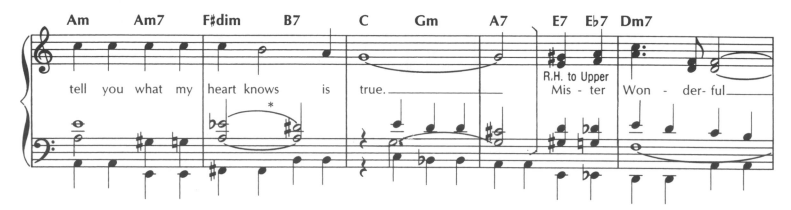

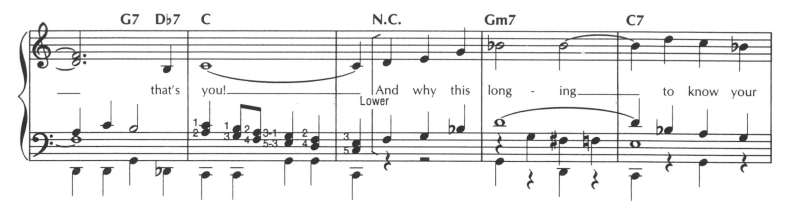

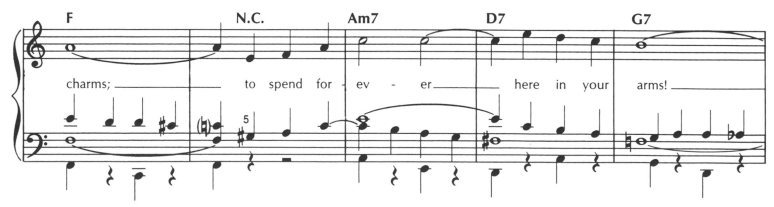

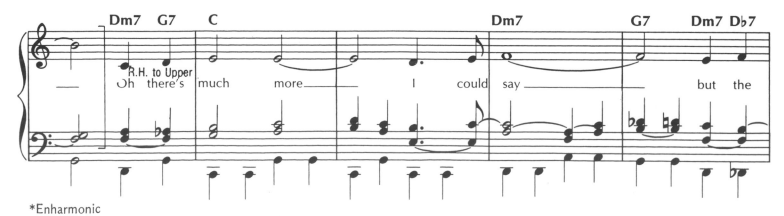

*Enharmonic

Oklahoma
from OKLAHOMA!

Electronic Organs

Upper: Flutes (or Tibias) 16', 8', 4', 2', 1'
         String 8'
Lower: Diapason 8', Flutes 8', 4'
         Reed 8'
Pedal: 16', 8', Sustain
Vib./Trem.: On, Full

Drawbar Organs

Upper: 80 8808 004
Lower: (00) 8654 222
Pedal: 68, Sustain
Vib./Trem.: On, Full

Lyrics by Oscar Hammerstein II
Music by Richard Rodgers

Lively

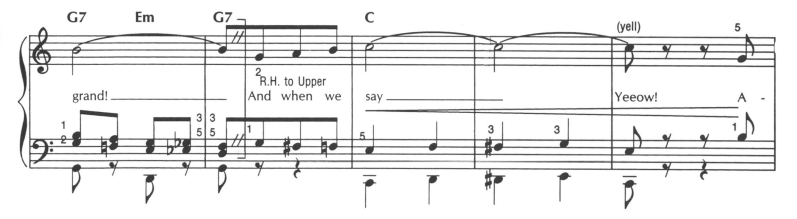

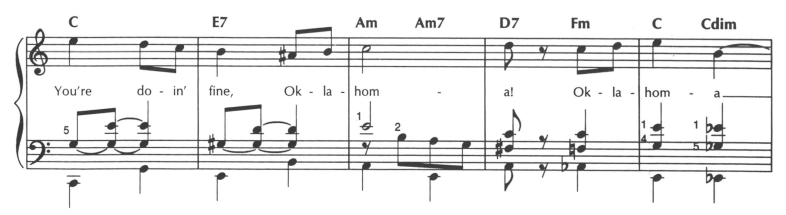

On the Street Where You Live

from MY FAIR LADY

Electronic Organs

Upper: Flutes (or Tibias) 16', 8', 4', 2⅔', 2'
Lower: Flutes 8', 4', String 8'
Pedal: 16', 8', Sustain
Vib./Trem.: On, Full

Drawbar Organs

Upper: 80 4800 080
Lower: (00) 8632 110
Pedal: 68, Sustain
Vib./Trem.: On, Full

Words by Alan Jay Lerner
Music by Frederick Loewe

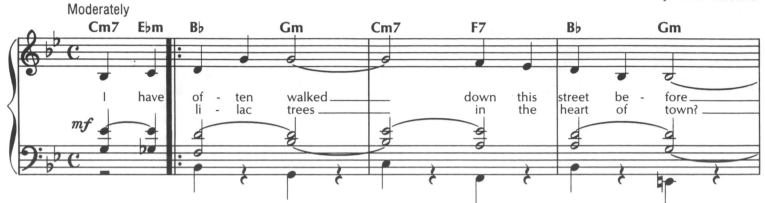

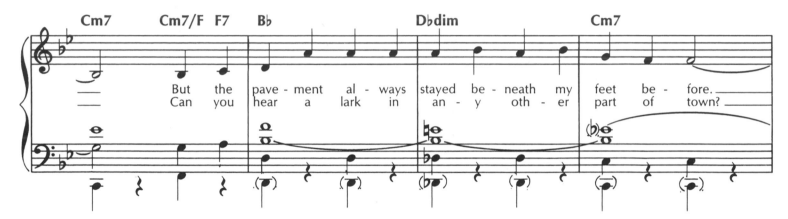

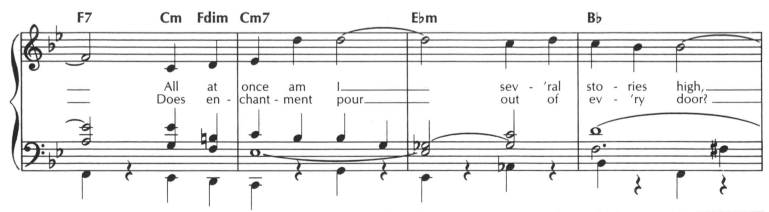

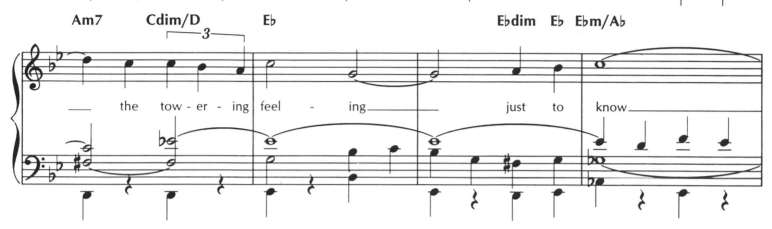

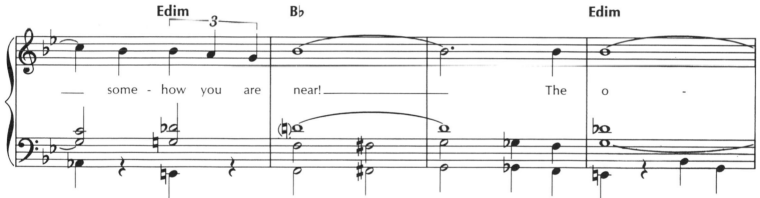

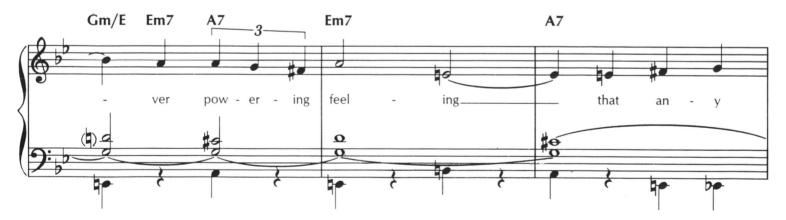

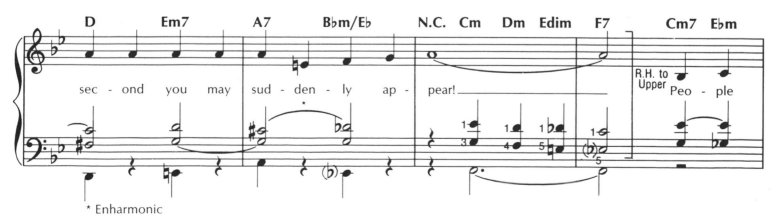

* Enharmonic

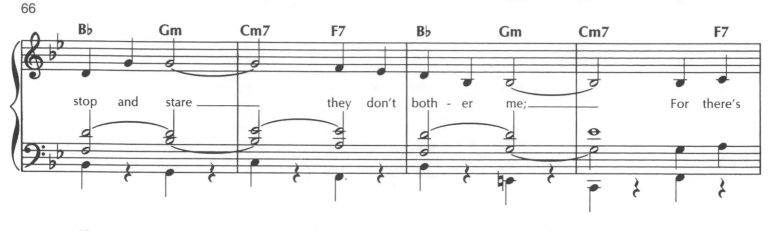

stop and stare ___ they don't both-er me; ___ For there's

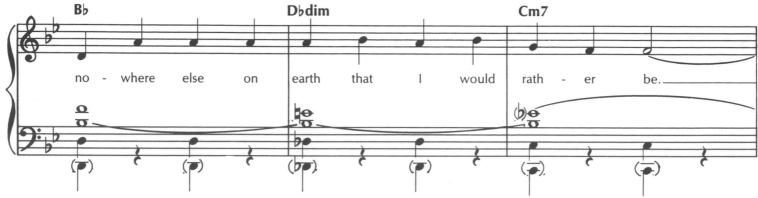

no - where else on earth that I would rath - er be. ___

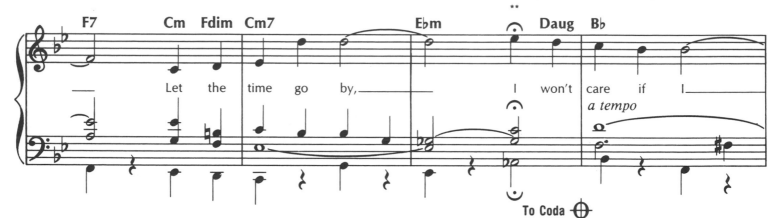

Let the time go by, ___ I won't care if I ___

a tempo

To Coda ⊕

can be here on the street where you live. ___

(2nd time, ritard)

D.S. al Coda

CODA   Freely, without a beat

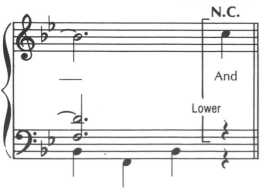

And

Lower

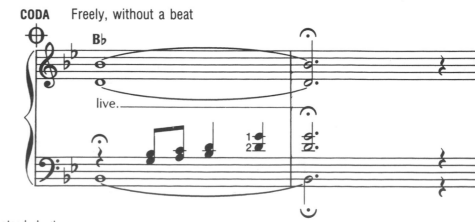

live. ___

** Fermata optional when playing with a steady beat

People

from FUNNY GIRL

Electronic Organs
Upper: Flute (or Tibia) 8'
       Long Sustain
Lower: Flute 8', Violin 8'
Pedal: 8'
Vib./Trem.:. Off

Tonebar Organs
Upper: 00 8000 000
Lower: (00) 5401 000
Pedal: 43
Vib./Trem.: Off

Words by Bob Merrill
Music by Jule Styne

Slowly, with feeling

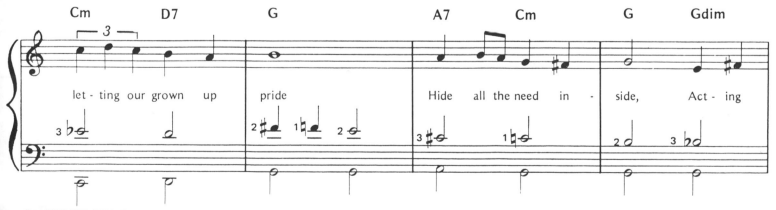

68

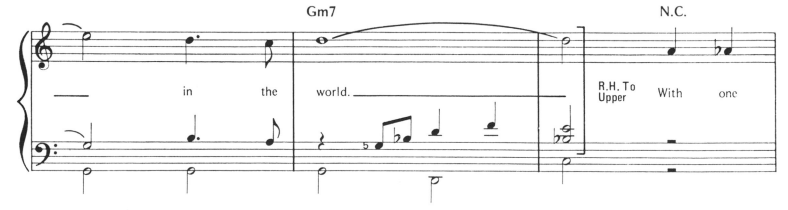

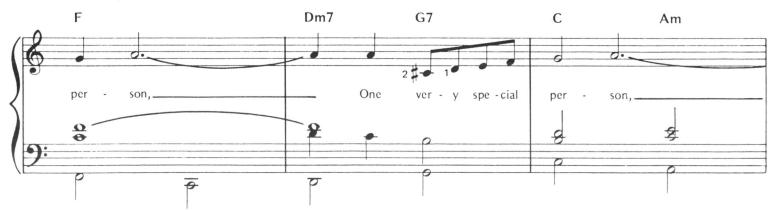

Thank Heaven for Little Girls

from GIGI

Electronic Organs

Upper: Flutes (or Tibias) 16′, 8′,
        String 4′
Lower: Flute 8′, Diapason 8′
Pedal: 16′, 8′
Vib./Trem.: On, Fast

Brightly

Tonebar Organs

Upper: 81 5505 004
Lower: (00) 7343 312
Pedal: 44
Vib./Trem.: On, Fast

Words by Alan Jay Lerner
Music by Frederick Loewe

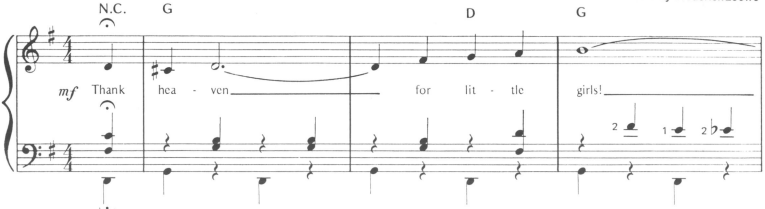

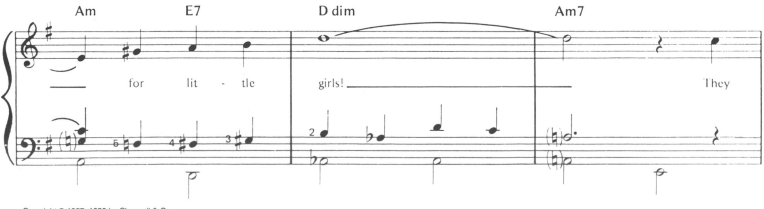

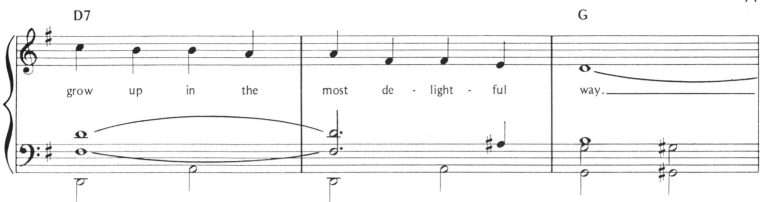

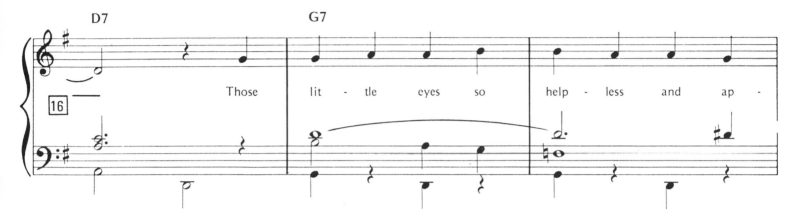

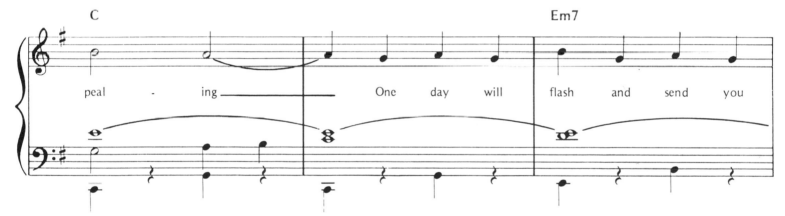

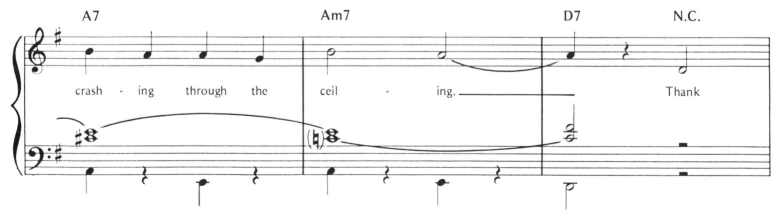

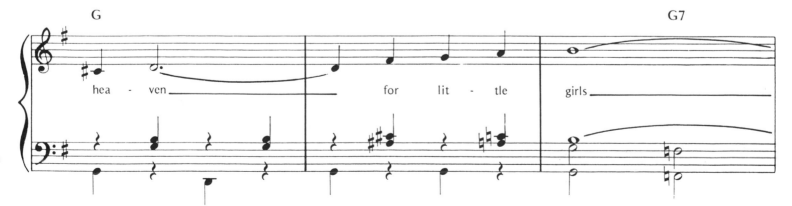

72

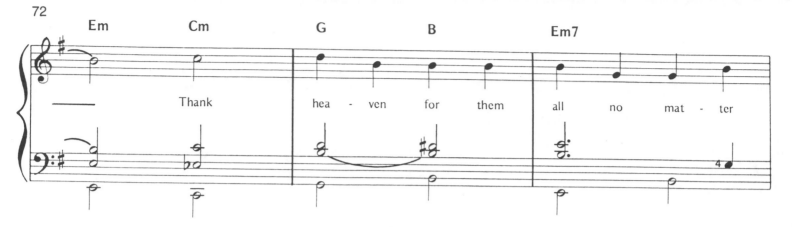

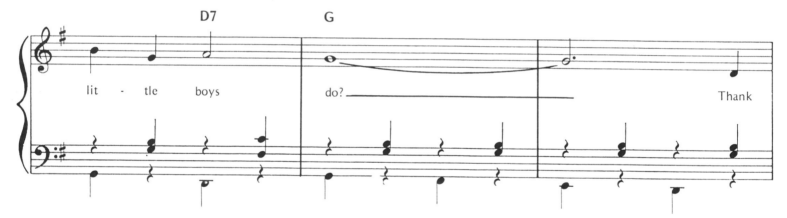

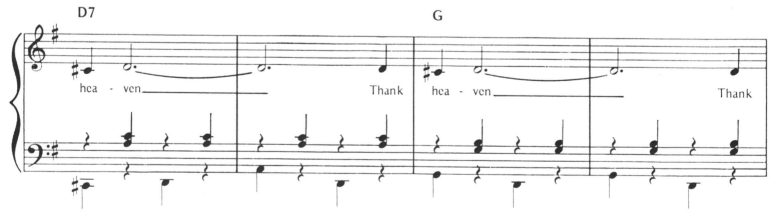

Wouldn't It Be Loverly

from MY FAIR LADY

Electronic Organs

Upper: Flutes (or Tibias) 8', 2'
Lower: Flutes 8', 4'
Pedal: String Bass
Vib./Trem.: On, Fast

Tonebar Organs

Upper: 00 7006 000
Lower: (00) 7600 000
Pedal: String Bass
Vib./Trem.: On, Fast

Words by Alan Jay Lerner
Music by Frederick Loewe

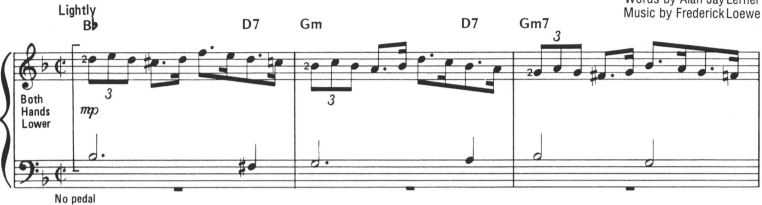

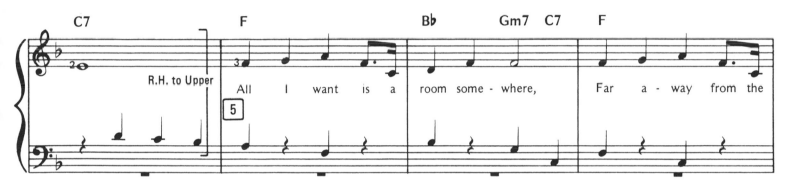

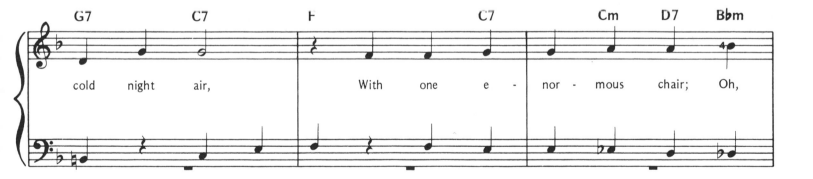

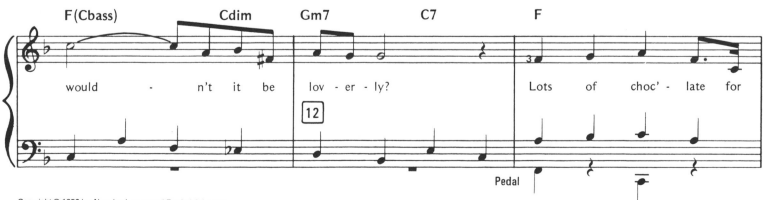

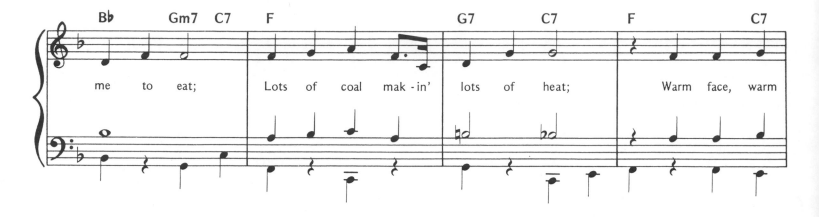

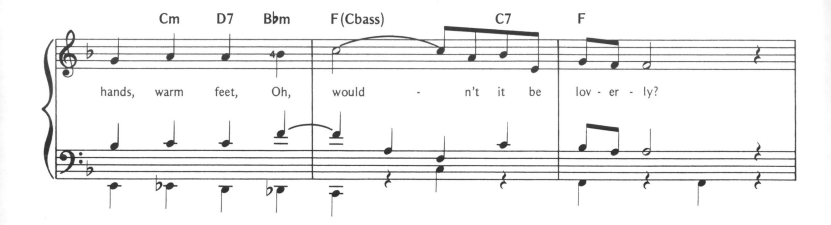

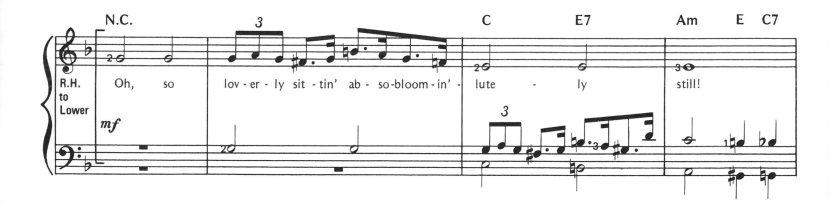

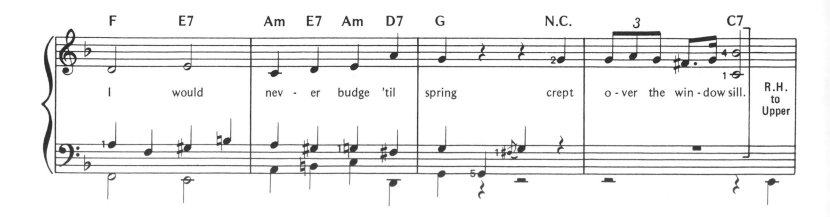

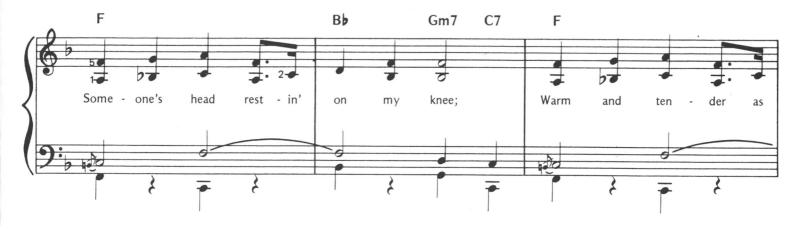

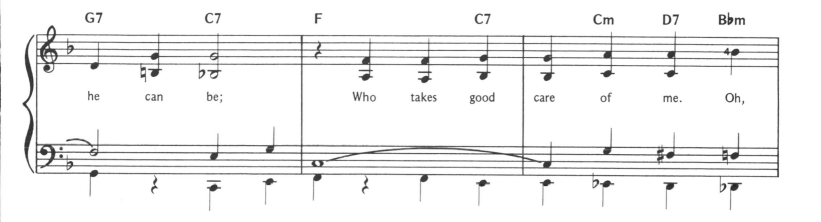

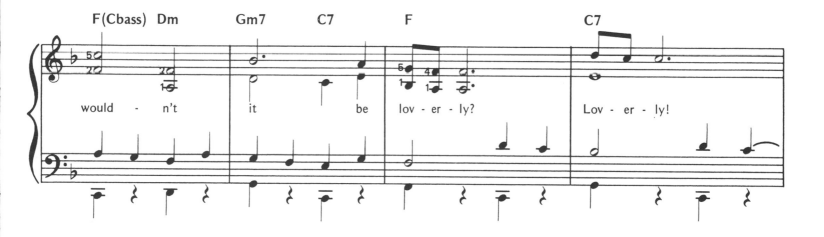

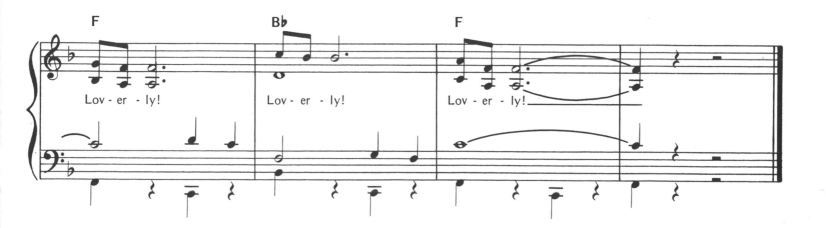

Wunderbar

from KISS ME, KATE

Electronic Organs

Upper: Flutes (or Tibias) 16', 8', 4', 2',
              String 8', Clarinet
Lower: Flute 8', Diapason 8', String 8'
Pedal: 16', 8'
Vib./Trem.: On, Fast

Tonebar Organs

Upper: 80 8104 103
Lower: (00) 7314 003
Pedal: 25
Vib./Trem.: On, Fast

Words and Music by
Cole Porter

Lively

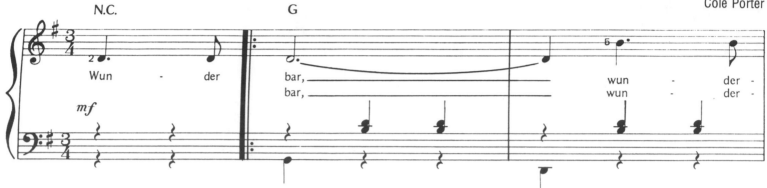

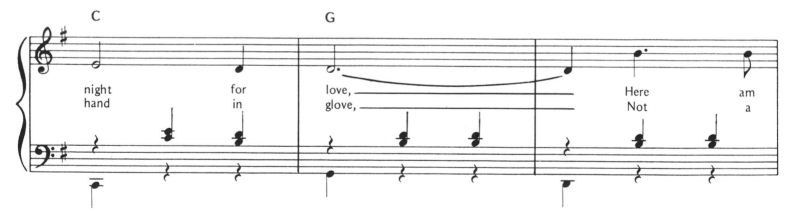

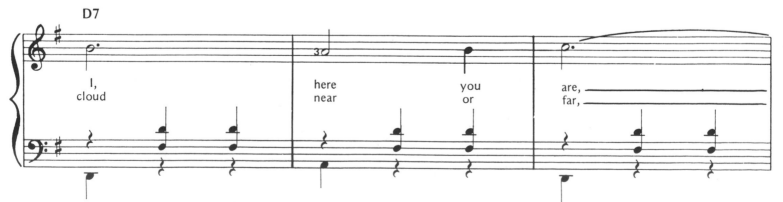

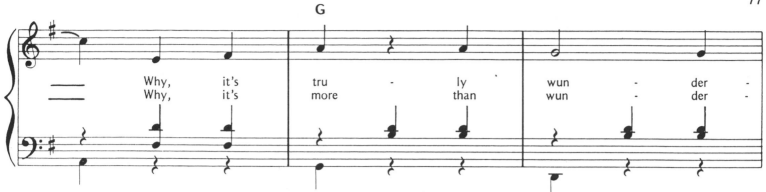

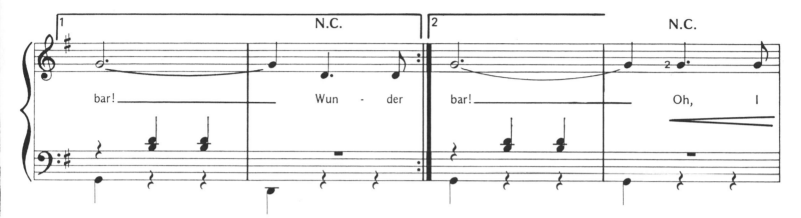

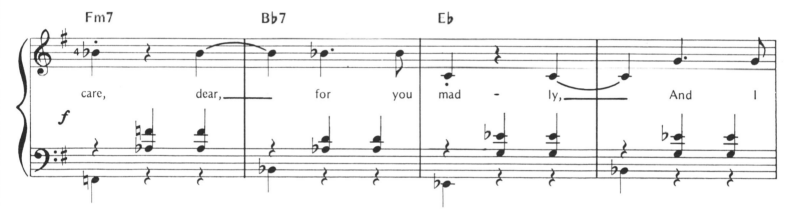

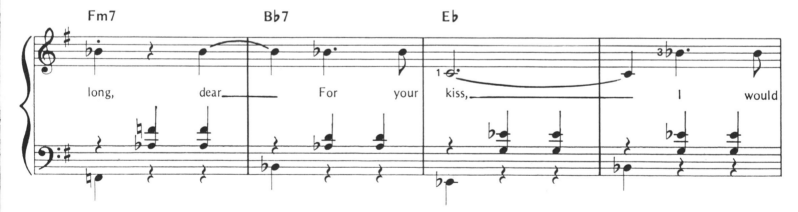

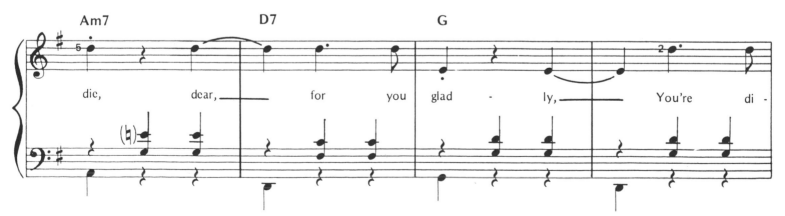

78

vine,   dear!____   And   you're   mine,   dear!____   Wun - der -

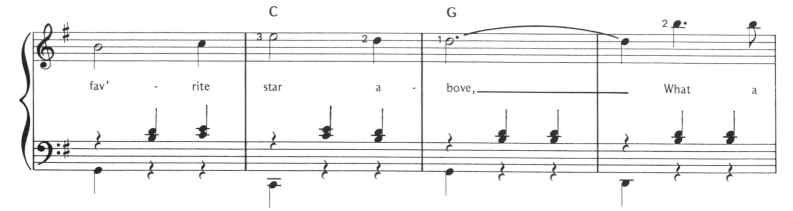

bar,_____   wun - der - bar!_____   There's   a

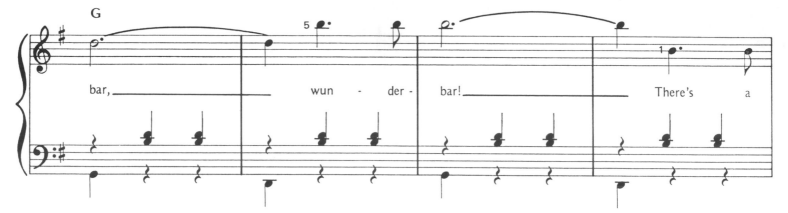

fav' - rite   star   a - bove,_____   What   a

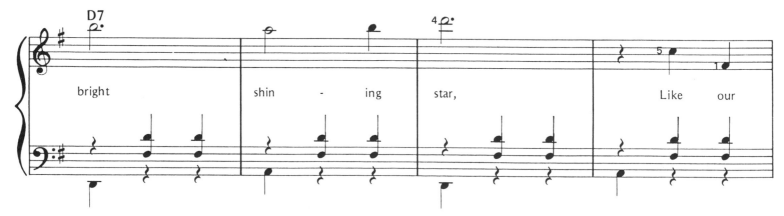

bright   shin - ing   star,   Like   our

love,   it's   wun - der - bar!_____